Reading this book is almost [like a] private coaching session with [...] exercises and anecdotes bring [to] life in ways that are practical a[nd I] will definitely be recommending [it to] anyone going through a transition or leading and organisation through one.

Shoshana Boyd Gelfand, Director of Leadership and Learning, Pears Foundation

So much is written about managing change and transitions in leadership literature, but so little is written about Endings - a critical stage of change. So here is an important, thought provoking book that deserves your attention. The authors highlight most leaders' capacity for new beginnings; new projects and exciting fresh starts (yup, guilty!), at the expense of attention given to 'endings', despite the emotion that can be wrapped up with this area. With their model of REAR (Reality, Emotion, Accomplishment, Rituals), they offer the leader a pragmatic guide through the field of Endings, and I sense this is going to be one of those (rare) leadership books I will return to, use, pass on and gift to others. Good Bye!

Dr Lucy Ryan, Executive Coach and Author, 'Revolting Women'

In one of our studies, in over 80% of cases when coaches and coachees looked back at an assignment, how they felt about it was directly related to how the ending was managed. Humans are in general very gauche about how we extricate ourselves from a meeting, whether it be a formal event or simply departing after a dinner party. The skill of good endings isn't taught in schools – but it should be! I am adding this title to my recommended reading list!

Professor David Clutterbuck

This is a refreshing book which challenges us to think differently about 'endings' and then equips us with tools to become better both professionally and personally. Both Alison and Lizzie guide us through some core principles and actionable insights which are thought provoking and inspiring. If you are looking for a practical tool to elevate your performance, this book is a must read.
Alice Mallen, UK and EMEA HR Director

Good Bye highlights a crucial yet often overlooked moment in leadership and organizational life. The thoughtfully crafted framework provides a practical and approachable model for navigating these pivotal transitions. The book offers valuable tools and actionable guidance that will enrich my leadership approach and will undoubtedly benefit leaders seeking to handle moments of parting with clarity and care.
Kirsty Devine, Head of US HR, Financial Times.

Good Bye is essential reading for every leader! In a VUCA world it is an essential guide on how to navigate change well, and urges leaders to recognize the many overlooked endings within their organisations – small transitions that, if ignored, can impede lasting progress. The over-riding theme of the book is the power of pause and intentionality and a human-centred approach to change. More than theory, *Good Bye* is grounded in deep insight, real-world examples and actionable tools that resonate far beyond the final page. An invaluable resource for leaders at every level.
Martina Doherty, Business Psychologist and Leadership Coach

As a funder I often see proposals for new projects and 'onboarding' volunteers but less attention is given to how a project ends and how a volunteer steps down. Perhaps the push for evaluation has taken our attention away from the more human-centred aspects of endings? The four steps are powerful in their simplicity and this book offers an essential toolkit for leaders who want to navigate endings with grace and intention.

Amy Braier, Director, Pears Foundation

Good Bye helped me guide a better ending for a long-standing team member. The REAR model helped me ensure they left understanding how valued they were, and prevented any potential negativity spreading within the team during their exit period.

I focussed on making sure their ending in the business was a positive one; to celebrate their achievements with the team and to recognize their contributions within the wider business. I framed every conversation around their time with the business as being both rewarding to them personally and also highly valued by the business. I encouraged them to view their time here as a stepping stone for their future career advancement rather than them consider it to be a failure and let them leave on a sour note. It worked; they left on a high and the remaining team have pushed on without losing any pace.

Commercial Director, Real Estate

I have benefitted greatly from the authors' experience and wisdom, while navigating 'Endings' on my personal career journey. This book will empower many more leaders to benefit, I will definitely be adding this to my recommended reading list for the HR and business leaders I work with.

**Nigel Standing, L&D Leader,
Fortune 250 organisation**

This insightful and accessible book by coaches Alison Lucas and Lizzie Bentley Bowers fills a crucial gap in leadership literature, shining a light on the often-overlooked importance of managing endings. While many leaders and organizations are well-versed in launching new initiatives, few are equipped to handle the emotional and practical complexities of closure – be it downsizing, merging teams, or ending a project. Lucas and Bowers challenge the 'new beginning' bias, offering a refreshingly empathetic perspective on the need for thoughtful endings. Their 4-step process is both straightforward and profound, guiding leaders in navigating transitions with emotional intelligence and respect. Packed with relatable scenarios and practical wisdom, this book is a must-read for leaders seeking to create lasting, positive change by honouring the full lifecycle of any endeavour, and essential reading for anyone guiding others through the complexities of organizational transformation.

**Marian Rosefield, Coach, Supervisor,
Researcher and Positive Psychology Practitioner**

Full of powerful insights and pragmatic help about an under-considered but vital area of leadership and, indeed, life management. A must read for all who lead and manage.
Christina Blacklaws, CEO Blacklaws Consulting, Campaigner, former President of the Law Society

GOOD

*Leading change
better by attending
to endings*

BYE

Lizzie Bentley Bowers & Alison Lucas

First published in Great Britain by Practical Inspiration Publishing, 2025

© Lizzie Bentley Bowers and Alison Lucas, 2025

The moral rights of the author have been asserted

ISBN 978-1-78-860728-5 (hardback)
      978-1-78-860729-2 (paperback)
      978-1-78-860731-5 (epub)
      978-1-78-860730-8 (Kindle)

All rights reserved. This book, or any portion thereof, may not be reproduced without the express written permission of the authors.

Every effort has been made to trace copyright holders and to obtain their permission for the use of copyright material. The publisher apologizes for any errors or omissions and would be grateful if notified of any corrections that should be incorporated in future reprints or editions of this book.

Want to bulk-buy copies of this book for your team and colleagues? We can customize the content and co-brand *Good Bye* to suit your business's needs.

Please email info@practicalinspiration.com for more details.

Practical Inspiration Publishing

MIX
Paper | Supporting responsible forestry
FSC® C013604

*In memory of our origin Giants
Dr. Peter Iredale and Jack Bentley*

*And for our Giants of the future
Ellen, Matthew and Ruth
Jack and Dylan*

π

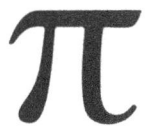

What we call the beginning is often the end
And to make an end is to make a beginning
The end is where we start from
We shall not cease from exploration
And the end of all our exploring
Will be to arrive where we started
And know the place for the first time

> T. S. Eliot, *Little Gidding*

Contents

A very good place to start *1*
Before we begin *15*

1	Beginning with Endings	17
2	The Four Steps – An introduction to REAR	51
3	You go first	69
4	Your first Steps	81

A half-time listening interlude *101*

5	Leading others	111
6	Step by step through the Steps	131
7	Brighter Beginnings	155
8	Good Bye, Dear Reader	157
9	Standing on the shoulders of Giants	159

Resources *175*
Exercises *181*
Endings stories *183*
Acknowledgements *185*
Index *189*
About the authors *195*

A very good place to start

There is a myriad of Endings every day in organizations.

The Oxford English Dictionary defines an Ending as 'the final part of something'. There is a starkness to this inevitable truth. Everything and everyone has a finite life and at some point this will come to an end. Endings will happen no matter what. Whether there is a Good Bye is optional.

What is a Good Bye? The definition of Good Bye is both a departing salutation and an acknowledgement of the fact that something is Ending. We have used it in its split format:

Good: to do something well, pay some attention

Bye: the Ritual of closing; a parting salutation.

If we pause from our multi-dimensional, relentless work as leaders and reflect on what Endings are occurring right now in our organization, there will be many. This is the missing jigsaw puzzle piece of leadership, and critically of leading change. In this Brittle, Anxious, Non-Linear and Incomprehensible (BANI) world, as described by Jamais Cascio, change is a constant Reality for organizations not only to survive, but to thrive. Change is constant, and change does not happen without Endings.

In calling this book *Good Bye* we are inviting you as leaders to think about closing well and paying attention to the Endings in your organization before you move forward. There is real finality and truth in the fact that an Ending ultimately means we are saying Good Bye in our heads and in our hearts. Work is a big part of people's lives, and during the course of our careers we are likely to repeatedly find ourselves saying Good Bye to something that might be quite significant to us, that might have been a major part of our identity. For example, when we retire from 'work', in other words, stop activity for economic gain, we are saying Good Bye to a long chapter of our existence. It might be intrinsically linked to who we are at an identity level: 'I used to be the CEO of …'. There are potentially multi-faceted Endings that come with retirement that we ignore to our detriment if we want our post-retirement life to have richness and purpose.

Endings come in all shapes and sizes. Some we have welcomed, some we dread. Some we have agency over, some are put upon us. Some we can influence, some we cannot. Sometimes we are the architect, sometimes others engineer the Ending, over which we have no choice or agency. Some are necessary, however much we wish they weren't, and as leaders we know it is the best path forward.

Some Endings are more obvious than others; some are bigger, some smaller. Some readily spring to mind, such as redundancies or office closures, and some are less obvious, like a promotion or a rebrand. When two teams are brought together, there are multiple Endings that are occurring both consciously and unconsciously. So many things change: the rhythms, routines, cultures, habits, physical spaces, relationships, conversations and more. In our keenness to create the new group and galvanize efficiencies, we may not attend to what has come to an end, or what sense of belonging is being lost.

Whenever you come across an exercise in this book, we invite you to adapt it to suit your way of learning or working, whilst keeping the essence of the task we're suggesting. We recommend keeping your notes on these exercises together as another useful exercise can be to review them and notice themes, connections and common threads.

Exercise 1: Bring current Endings into focus

Ask yourself:
- How many Endings am I experiencing right now?
- How much attention am I paying to Ending well?

We suspect this might be an area to which you have not paid much attention. If that is the case, rest assured that you are not alone. It is a neglected, dusty corner of leadership which has never really had a light shone on it; a blind spot in organizational development and design. When we developed this work and turned to our leadership bookshelves, there was barely a mention of it in a chapter, let alone any practical guidance. We were curious about that, and by having chosen this book, we hope you are too.

Leaders know how to start things, a burning platform to launch an initiative, a project plan with milestones, a compelling vision of the future, ambition, drive and energy with meaning and goals. We know often what is not working and what needs to be changed. There is something exciting and energizing about the future; something new, something better. Yet in this desire to move forward, to create the new, we sometimes rush towards it, without thinking about what might be Ending.

And even if as leaders we are aware of an Ending, that does not necessarily translate to dealing with it. In our experience leaders are often reluctant to acknowledge an Ending or they get caught between how they are feeling and their role as a leader in a way that is not useful. In some cases, leaders might avoid the Ending altogether, for example by not letting someone go, or not restructuring a team.

We believe the ability to pause is a vital leadership skill; to consider the Endings that you may be experiencing yourself or the Endings for which you are the architect for others. It is more often than not an uncomfortable place to be, as it may involve complex Emotions, and vulnerabilities. Most leaders are not taught how to sit with that discomfort. Nor are they taught how to navigate their own relationship with Endings, for themselves, in order to then be able to confidently lead others. This is a blight on the leadership education system. Researcher and author Brené Brown brought vulnerability into our leadership vocabulary; now we wish to help you navigate a vulnerable area with some grace and ease. We offer you a way to start to consider this deep, important and stretching area of human existence and leadership. We offer an opportunity to include Good Byes when you are thinking about the leader you want to grow into.

A leader who is more aware of their own patterns, strengths and development areas, with the emotional intelligence to lead change effectively, is the only leader who will be successful in today's world. Leaders cannot wholly outsource the navigation of Endings, including the resulting change and difficult conversations, to specialist departments.

A Good Bye does not mean it is all neatly wrapped up and all parties are happy. This is not always happily-ever-after territory, nor is it wishful thinking. This is about doing the work to best support yourself and those you lead through what we call 'the messy stuff'. There may be many Emotions attached to an Ending, and we may not be able to resolve or fix it. However, if we have owned our own part and led others emotionally through it then we have ensured that there is more choice as to how to move forward. It does not have to be good to be a Good Bye.

Throughout this book we will be sharing examples of both poorly managed Endings and examples of Endings that are managed sensitively and professionally. Here is a story we have heard a version of many, many times. We know it's highly likely that you'll have seen or felt a version of this too. Notice how it feels to read it. You may want to note your thoughts and feelings in the margin or in your ongoing notes as you are reading.

An all too common tale

William had been working as a Chief People Officer (CPO) with European-wide responsibility in a multinational organization. He had been head-hunted into the role, and in three years had exceeded the targets that had been set when he was brought in to the company. William was well liked and respected by his Executive (Exec) team peers and the teams that reported into them. A change of personal circumstance meant that William wanted a role with less travel abroad. He took another CPO role based closer to home and with less international travel. From the point that he resigned onwards the relationships with the rest of the Exec team materially shifted. It was clear they had seen this as a betrayal and shut William out, making it clear that his view on strategic priorities was no longer of interest.

Three weeks into the new role, someone asked William at a social event how the new job was going. Initially he spoke about how well the new job was going and how he was enjoying finding his feet. William then spoke at length about how hurt, upset, undermined, frustrated and disrespected he had felt during his exit from his previous organization. He felt the company had seen it as an act of disloyalty, turning on him. He was deeply hurt that none of the Exec team had acknowledged his last day, nor did they thank him or wish him well. He found himself playing his perceived injustice over and over again in his mind.

Exercise 2: What is resonating for you?

- What thoughts and feelings came up as you were reading this?
- What are you reminded of from your own experience?

Our hope in writing this book is that it prompts you to get curious about your own patterns of behaviour around Endings; we hope it will give you a simple, yet powerful, framework to help navigate these patterns for yourself and with your team. It will help you:

- Realize where you may feel vulnerable
- Get clear on the full Reality of the situation you are leading

- Identify how you are feeling, and what might be going on for others
- Ensure that you don't lose sight of all that has gone before in the messiness that is an Ending
- Honour the final Good Bye in a ceremony or Ritual
- Put yourself in a much stronger position to extract the learning from an Ending and carry that forward.

As senior leaders in our previous careers, and subsequently as coaches, we have observed the impact of poorly managed Endings reverberating through the systems we work in.

In response to this we developed our hub of resources, Endings for Beginnings (which you can now find at GoodByeCoach.co.uk) – a methodology to help leaders stop avoiding and start attending to Endings, which was the origin of this book.

We wholeheartedly believe that the organizational world would be a kinder, better, more productive place if 10% of the energy and effort that is put into new Beginnings was orientated to acknowledging the Endings. We look forward to helping you achieve this.

How to use this book

1. We are practitioners. This work is born out of practice underscored by both modern and ancient wisdom and born out of our work with our leaders. So please use it to enhance your leadership practice. Always start with yourself. You cannot lead another through change well without being clear on your thoughts and feelings. You may be the architect of change and you may not. Get clear, and then turn to those you lead, and what they

might need from you. Start slowly, use this to guide your awareness for yourself; from there, look at how you lead others through Endings.
2. Work safely. Endings are complex, messy and often bound up in all sorts of beliefs, disappointments, conflicting Emotions, losses and grief. In our experience, some people have found these exercises uncomfortable. If you notice that you are feeling discomfort, remember that discomfort can be a positive sign that you are touching upon something important. If you sense this, you may want to take a short break and then return to the exercise in order to give yourself additional time to explore whatever important feeling or insight is causing the discomfort. But our experience suggests that noticing discomfort is often the first step towards a profound realization. So, start slowly, and boundary the work. If it brings up stuff that feels bigger than you can process on your own, seek support. Be kind to yourself.
3. Give this time and space. Give others time and space. This work will draw on many of your skills as a leader. Perhaps most importantly, the skill of listening. Be prepared to listen to yourself, and to others.
4. This book isn't a one-size-fits-all, and we don't expect everyone who reads it to use it the same way. Feel free to do less of some things, and more of others. Feel free to adapt and adjust exercises to make them comfortable for you and your teams. We have capitalized the Four REAR Steps (Reality, Emotions, Accomplishments and Ritual) through the book for ease of reference, but that doesn't mean you have to use these in your own work or as you work with others. For example, it might feel more comfortable to think of emotions with a small 'e'

as a quiet acknowledging of feelings. Ritual with a small 'r' might be a brief, deliberate pause to mark a moment. Adapt the work to work for you.

5. If you want to know more about the works that have influenced us and helped us shape our practice, please turn to the final chapter 'Standing on the Shoulders of Giants'. Here you will get a brief introduction to our Giants, why their work is important to *Good Bye* and where you can find out more. When we refer to these Giants you will see the π symbol in the margin. π

6. Where examples are given they are either materially changed amalgamations of several experiences we have had, or are examples that we have been given explicit permission to share. Any similarity to your own stories, or stories you have heard, is purely coincidental and is an indication of how often Endings go unattended.

7. Look around for examples. The lack of guidance on Endings means that when organizations and leaders end well, which many do, they may not be aware of how they did it or the impact it had. The opportunity for it to be something to be learned from and repeat was missed. As you read this book, we encourage you to start noticing more about the Endings around you. It will be clear when they are managed poorly. But we also hope you can use this work to be more alert to when it is done well so that you can learn from that too.

Being practitioners at heart, if what we do or say does not have an impact, we change our approach. We also know that a model, process or tool helps guide, bring structure and a place to start. In our leadership conversations with our clients, we help them get clarity, explore options, uncover hidden assumptions, plan a way forward, uncover how they are feeling, share what their fear might be and hold them accountable to what they want to achieve.

Let's look then at an Ending done well.

I loved you. You loved me. We'll all be OK.

Jürgen Klopp left his role as Manager of Liverpool Football Club in 2024; there was, rightly, a celebration of his achievements at the club. If you watch his final interview on the Liverpool FC YouTube channel, you can see all Four Steps of the approach to Ending well that we are about to share with you.[1] We love the way this interview looks back at the results and both the highs and lows of his time as Manager. It explores the impact of his leaving on himself, players and fans. The conversation then turns towards the future for the club and for Klopp personally. It is an example of how by ensuring that an individual whose work has been appreciated has a fitting Ending, so much more can ripple out. There is full acknowledgement of the Reality (he didn't shy away from talking through the difficulties and challenges of his tenure as well as the successes), the Emotions, the Accomplishments and the beautiful Rituals. One such Ritual was a book of comments of appreciation from fans, staff and players alike. It includes looking forward to what's next too. By contrast with some of the examples you'll encounter in this book he says, 'I can't wait for life, for life after the career'.

---

[1] www.youtube.com/watch?v=-dcbhxJ2lzw

The threads of an Ending can create knots and tangles in our teams, our organizations and even within ourselves.

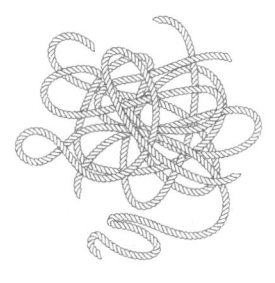

This work is about understanding these knots, untangling them and releasing the tension into a stronger, unencumbered rope – the threads all released to where they naturally belong, and where they can then combine to strengthen each other.

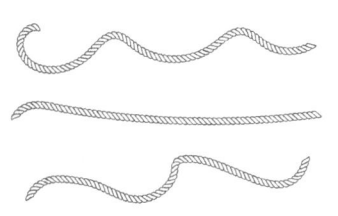

We have taken wisdom from our learning, our observations and experiences with our clients to put together a simple model or guide rail. This guide rail will help you walk through an Ending and put it where it needs to be – in the past, fully acknowledged, freeing the present and the future for what can come next.

You can see how once the knots are untangled and the threads separated out, a Good Bye flows into a Hello with more ease, more clarity and more energy.

saying Good Bye ⟿⟿⟿⟿⟿ saying Hello to today

The question we asked ourselves as we worked on this with our clients was how can we help leaders to untangle this for themselves? From here, we designed our Four Steps, designed to support you in leading yourself and others through Good Byes: Reality, Emotions, Accomplishments and Ritual.

REAR

- RITUAL
- ACCOMPLISHMENTS
- EMOTIONS
- REALITY

Looking back to look forward

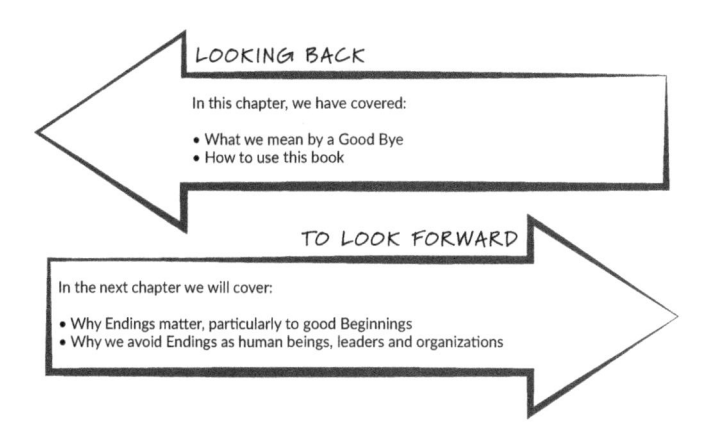

LOOKING BACK

In this chapter, we have covered:

- What we mean by a Good Bye
- How to use this book

TO LOOK FORWARD

In the next chapter we will cover:

- Why Endings matter, particularly to good Beginnings
- Why we avoid Endings as human beings, leaders and organizations

But before we begin, some important guidance…

Before we begin

Before we begin, here are some important acknowledgements about what this book is **not** intended for.

Death

The ultimate Ending is the death or passing away of a loved one, a friend or a colleague. As a leader you may have responsibilities in dealing with compassionate leave for a direct report, be experiencing your own grief as it impacts you at work or even be dealing with the death of a colleague. This book is not designed, nor does it equip you, for the sensitive, and often specialist skills needed to navigate this for yourself and others. For more advice and guidance in this area, you could refer to the work of Kathryn Mannix, Julia Samuel and Dr Lucy Hone – full details are in the Resources list at the end of this book.

Denial and timing

Part of the grieving process associated with death, or any loss, can be denial.

Whilst denial at an organizational level may be viewed simplistically as not useful, it may well serve a purpose for the individual, team and organization, helping them adapt over time. For example, it can act as a shield that buffers from the immediacy of the Ending. It can prevent emotional flooding and allow for gradual adjustment. It provides time to process and a plan to go forward.

When denial shows up in an organizational Ending, a significant sense of loss and grief may have been experienced. As you work through this book, if what you are experiencing is that you, or those you lead, are not moving out of denial, tread carefully. When leading others, tread particularly carefully when an individual does not have agency, and the Reality feels daunting.

You may need to allow more time for coming to terms with a new Reality. We are not saying rush headlong into processing an Ending using our Four Steps. You may need to keep the Reality at bay to keep functioning in your day-to-day role, or to protect yourself whilst making or implementing tough decisions. You may need to seek support.

Pause. Choose your moment. When you, and others you want to share this work with, are nearer to acceptance and ready to face the Reality, and you are confident you are ready as a leader, only then take the first Step.

Trauma

If in reading this book, or doing any of this work, feelings of trauma arise, or resurface, we encourage you to stop and seek support.

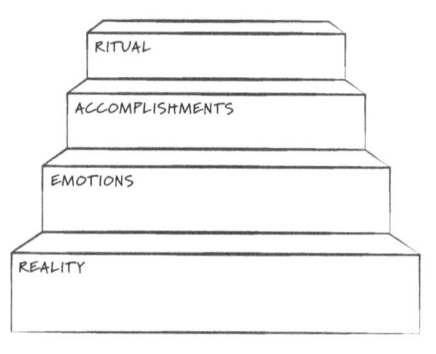

```
                    ┌──────────────────┐
                    │ RITUAL           │
              ┌─────┴──────────────────┴─────┐
              │ ACCOMPLISHMENTS              │
        ┌─────┴──────────────────────────────┴─────┐
        │ EMOTIONS                                 │
  ┌─────┴──────────────────────────────────────────┴─────┐
  │ REALITY                                              │
  └──────────────────────────────────────────────────────┘
```

Chapter 1

Beginning with Endings

As we've already seen, Endings are a constant and significant part of working life. Iona Lawrence, Co-Founder of The Decelerator, who is one of our fellow travellers and thought leaders in the world of Endings for organizations says, 'Embracing endings is essential to thoughtful and visionary leadership in civil society'. Why is it then that leaders and organizations put relatively little thought, energy and resource towards paying attention to them?

> **Exercise 3: Beginnings get a lot of attention**
>
> Take a moment to consider what, as an organization, you spend on Beginnings. Things like inductions, new initiatives, re-branding, product launches, etc.
> - What do you invest in terms of money and time on new starts?
> - What do you invest in terms of energy and Emotion on new starts?

The investment in how someone begins a new role ensures they are ready to make a positive contribution, and that investment is visible in everything from interviews to onboarding processes. Other examples include roadshows to socialize and share visions and new goals or to attract new talent; or new products being designed and marketed, and the 'launch' of a team, project or product.

We tend to see less investment in Endings. Not only that, the impact of that lack of investment is unclear. And herein lies the rub. It is a more hidden, subtle and pernicious cost.

> *Systems don't tolerate 'moving on', 'forgetting', or otherwise excluding …yet organisations around the world still give people more to leave than they did to join, believing that this will help them leave the organisational memory. It has exactly the opposite effect.*
>
> John Whittington

This effect is really hard to see, let alone quantify.

> ***Consider:*** *What, then, do you think the cost is, and why does paying attention to Endings matter?*

In this chapter we look at what the individual and organizational impact of missed or rushed Endings is, and why it is that we avoid or hurry through them.

Why Endings matter

Everything we are about to share with you illustrates the impact that well-managed Endings could have on profit, results and wellbeing. Attending to Endings creates a whole host of opportunities to save money and to create a happier workforce.

Why?

- **Lessons are learned.** Organizations waste millions on launching new initiatives, only to do it again a few years later. For reasons they haven't been able to decipher, something hasn't fully landed nor has it shifted into future work. Imagine if a team that has been working on a project or product (which has failed) then works through their Reality, Emotions, Accomplishments and closes with a Ritual. Having disentangled themselves from the project, they are in a much better position to learn further lessons and not repeat the same mistakes.
- **Reduced people cost.** Imagine if trust and team spirit is grown as a result of people naturally leaving an organization. Turnover of staff may decrease whilst focus and discretionary performance increase. We have seen many examples of the high cost of recruitment processes into very senior roles, where the new executive struggles to assimilate into the role and subsequently leaves, only for the organization to have to go through the whole recruitment expense again. So often, this is not about the ability or skill of the leaders, it's about the way the Endings and Beginnings were managed.
- **Perspective.** Imagine if an Ending has been well handled, and left cleanly in the past. The organization is more likely to be looking up and out instead of back and down. We can't help wondering how different it might have been for companies that struggled to look to the future, ultimately leading to the end of the company, if they had been equipped to pay full attention to what was Ending. Do you remember Blockbuster video? (Readers like us of a certain age will, but some may need to look them up!)

Had Blockbuster said a proper and timely Good Bye to the end of an era in order to embrace the next one, where they kept some of what they did but let other things go, perhaps things might have been different for them.

- **Increased opportunities for equity.** The Decelerator Helpline shared with us that their experience is that the status quo with endings is inequitable. Endings are managed in ways that all too often put the greatest burden on those who arguably should be carrying less. In our overlooking of endings generally, unequal systems and patterns can continue and prosper when endings present opportunities to deconstruct the inequity in organisations and society that are no longer serving us. 'Brighter Beginnings' are an opportunity to redistribute power, leave things behind (for example norms, behaviours, ways of work, artefacts) and intentionally create fairer and more equitable beginnings.
- **Certainty.** When Endings are acknowledged and managed it creates more certainty. Certainty is calming. It's the solid ground from which we can plan. One of the benefits of being more open to, and more able to account for, everyday Endings is being able to see the larger scale Endings coming. It would be easy to assume that it is demotivating to think about the end when you are Beginning. On the contrary, we have seen how startups that are really clear on their exit plan, or charities with a finite amount of timing and/or funding, are much better equipped to account for and plan for their Ending. In acknowledging the certainty of the Ending throughout, rather than avoiding it, they are

not caught out by the Ending. They don't rush through it when time is running out.

Let's expand on some of these reasons why attending to Endings matters.

Endings can leave scars

For a live illustration of why Endings matter, ask anyone this question: 'Have you ever left a role in a way that didn't feel good?' If the answer is yes, now ask them to tell you more about it, and see what happens.

This tends to be one of those open-the-flood-gates moments. You get what we call a full-colour tale, and it doesn't matter whether it's an event that took place recently or decades ago, the plot, sub-plots, characters, settings and details will all still be there. Because Ending well, and by extension Ending badly, matters to people, and it stays with them.

The chances are you have one of those tales to tell yourself too, maybe more than one. We certainly have. In our early conversations on this subject, we shared our own experiences of difficult Endings and noticed not only the detail we could still recall, but how freshly we still felt Emotions, how hard it was to turn our thinking to something else, and how energy sapping it was. A sense of unfinished business or injustice lingers, and it can be distracting at best, and draining at worst.

In our experience, when a difficult or painful Ending has not been properly processed, the Emotions can still be raw long after the leader has seemingly moved on.

🌀 *Too easily discarded*

Kim had been a senior procurement officer for a large Fast Moving Consumer Goods (FMCG) company. She had worked her way up the organization and had 20 years' service. She had over the years been a steady performer, loyal and hard working. When her organization went through a companywide talent review she was in the bottom quartile. She was subsequently called in to her line manager's office, with an HR officer. She was told she was being made redundant and was then escorted out of the building. When we met Kim five years later, the story was still Full Colour, and the scars were still very apparent. Her behaviour was impacted in that she did not give her loyalty fully to her new organization, for want of being hurt and blindsided so catastrophically again.

Whilst this story has been told from Kim's perspective, it's worth noting that the scars are not just inflicted on those who have left, but also for those who may have been the instigators, the implementors or the witnesses.

Endings impact relationships and behaviours

When leaders are paying attention to Endings they are paying attention to people, processes and the systemic[2]

---

[2] 'Systemic' refers to issues, processes or changes that are deeply embedded in and affect the entire structure, culture and operations of the organization, rather than being isolated or surface-level.

health of the organization. Paying attention to Endings also involves having perspective on the past, present and future. All this enables individuals and teams to perform better and work productively in the present.

When the Ending is missed or rushed, the different experiences of the individuals within the team are either not spoken about or are spoken about in private conversations that can lead to rifts and silos. There is an impact on confidence in self and each other, on trust, on energy and on being fully present and engaged with the here and now.

This isn't always obvious.

Building belonging

Itsuki could not understand why their team, created by merging two teams that seemed to be collaborating so well to start with, over time became fractious. There was investment at the start in opportunities for the teams to get to strategize and prioritize collaboratively. Even though members of both the previous teams were combined across all projects, old silos seemed to still surface within those teams. Through exploration and conversation with us, Itsuki realized that whilst the combined teams worked well together initially, they did not play together. Sports teams and social events were organized and attended in their former teams. The odd bit of gossip at those events, when none of the 'other team' was present, had a knock on to casual conversations in the office and ultimately to a sense that their unity was superficial.

> *There was a creeping impact from the way team members held on to old loyalties and close relationships. It was important for new relationships and cohesions to form, in order to build a new, united team.*
>
> *Itsuki then commissioned a team Away Day to help the team recognize and bridge their divisions. We invited them to divide back into their original teams and work through the Ending of that team. Both teams paid attention to what had come to an end and, by doing so, when we then invited them to come together as the merged team, they were more present and able to engage in moving forward together. This simple and powerful intervention had a significant impact on the trust and relationship of the team. Old silos made way for an energized, integrated team.*

Endings are rife with opportunities to build or diminish trust

You will not find a single book, article or podcast on thriving, psychologically safe teams that does not reference trust as an essential component. We all know that feeling when we are seeming to the outside world as though we are fully engaged (indeed we are working productively and getting things done) but that is underpinned by a sense of unease that impacts our attention, energy and confidence. In turn, this impacts the decisions we make, the conversations we have and our relationships within and between teams.

An example of a performance management system that doesn't build trust is that of Forced Ranking, delightfully summarized by many as 'yank and rank', which was popularized in the 1980s and 1990s by the legendary Jack Welsh of General Electric.

It has previously been used by Microsoft, GSK and many other organizations, and is still used by some organizations today.

The organization ranks all the employees, with a small percentage being deemed top performers, the majority in the middle and the bottom 10% exited. Hence the 'yank'. It systematically identifies and takes out the bottom 10% of employees based on performance. This has many issues if you look at it through the lens of Ending well. On top of encouraging individualism not collaboration, Edward E. Lawler III explores in 'The Folly of Forced Ranking' how it also leads to behaviours where managers who are asked to rank their teams find ways of circumventing the system in order to keep favourites, or use the system to get rid of people rather than developing the team. It also becomes trickier year on year, as employees see it coming and change their behaviour in order to survive. Those behaviours are not necessarily in the long-term interests of the organization, or those individuals. In our opinion this type of public cull across the board based on a known ranking is humiliating for the individual and is at best a mixture of relief and difficulty for the leaders. It's a system that is rife with issues and is no substitute for good leadership and progressive people development. We are not saying performance doesn't matter, quite the contrary, but forced ranking is unlikely to lead to a Good Bye for any party.

Endings can light up our threat responses

The brain experiences the workplace first and foremost as a social system... people who feel betrayed or unrecognised at work, experience it as a neural impulse, as powerful and painful as a blow to the head.

David Rock

π David Rock's highly regarded SCARF model, first published in 2008, is a simple, brain-based model, which is especially relevant to leaders and managers. This model can be used as a way of understanding the impact of both behaviour and decisions. It is a useful resource for understanding why Endings can be so emotionally hijacking. The science behind it explains that the brain will make us behave in ways that try to minimize perceived threats and maximize rewards. If a person feels that they are being threatened, their primitive emotional brain will work quickly to protect them and, in doing so, will reduce their capacity for rational thought, decision-making and collaboration. Rock identifies five domains of experience that typically activate strong threat and reward responses. You can think of each domain like a button that can be pushed by something someone else says or does, by the environment or by something that happens. When the button gets pushed, our responses become less thoughtful, less about the here and now, instead becoming emotional and more about how we felt about, and reacted to, past experiences. Notice how an Ending in an organization could push one, some or all of these buttons.

SCARF (Status, Certainty, Autonomy, Relatedness, Fairness)

1. **Status** is about relative importance to others and is a significant driver of workplace behaviour. Your brain

is constantly monitoring your status in any group. This is why for many of us, our job title matters. It says something about our status. Many organizations try to create flat structures, however there is a Reality to the fact that we are wired to notice, and respond to, our sense of hierarchy. We might say we're not bothered by status but dig into that a little and people tend to notice that they do have feelings about their status or perceived status, as well as views on other people's status.

2. **Certainty** is how sure we are about what is coming next. It's about being able to predict the future. Sometimes, the only certainty we have is being certain about what we don't know, and that is still important to acknowledge. Often when it comes to Endings, there are unknowns beyond that Ending, as well a lack of clarity about the full Reality of what has ended. So, creating certainty about what is finishing and what is starting can be very settling. For all of us, clarity and certainty are important, and an Ending, even one that is positive, creates a level of uncertainty.

3. **Autonomy** is about having a sense of control in what is happening. It is about agency and choice. When we have talked about whether you are the architect of an Ending, or on the receiving end, it is the autonomy button that is being pushed. The brain likes to predict and have a say over the future and the part we play in it.

4. **Relatedness** gives a sense of safety with others. We are social animals, and we naturally form social groups and build relationships. The need to belong is one of the most fundamental of human needs. Being in a group with mutual trust builds a barrier against the unknown. When you connect with people you like or trust you get

a decrease in the stress hormone cortisol and more of the feel-good hormones oxytocin and dopamine.

5. **Fairness** is the perception of fair exchange between people. It is about the belief that there is equity of experience and opportunity. Everyone likes to feel that they have been dealt with in a fair manner. This is a nuanced and complex domain that requires sensitivity to and appreciation of protected characteristics[3] and lived experiences. Perceptions of fairness will be impacted by people's lives and experiences.

Endings, as we can see, are prime territory for threat responses. We often talk with our clients about the threat or stress that is created by an Ending. Some stress is more immediate and obvious. Some is less obvious and ongoing, and the kind you only really notice when it stops. We call it the low hum – like that low hum of a computer, lighting and general office noise that you only really 'hear' when it is suddenly all switched off.

What happens, then, when we are under threat? How do we respond? Research into trauma responses has given us an understanding of our responses in a way that is familiar to many of us as 'Fight/Flight/Freeze'. Extreme or chronic stress has an impact on our brains and our nervous system causes us to behave in ways that are designed to keep us safe and minimize the harm that can be done to us. Those

---

[3] In the UK, protected characteristics are specific attributes safeguarded against discrimination under the Equality Act 2010. These include age, disability, gender reassignment, marriage and civil partnership, pregnancy and maternity, race, religion or belief, sex and sexual orientation.

instinctive behaviours, however, aren't always entirely useful. What kept us safe when our brains were developing in ancient times, for example navigating threats from sabre tooth tigers or being excluded from the tribe, isn't necessarily what we need to manage the real or perceived threats we experience at work. When our brains aren't clear on the difference, it can lead to difficulties when we can find ourselves responding in ways that aren't necessarily appropriate or proportionate. To complicate this further, we are often doing a lot of this unconsciously. We are perceiving, processing and reacting to the threat without being fully aware of it.

Here are some examples of threat response reactions in a work situation:

RESPONSE	obvious		less obvious
FIGHT counter attack	Lashing out verbally or physically	Continual disagreement without explanation; entrenched in a view	Sarcasm; eye rolling
FLIGHT/FLEE run away	Resign	Absence	Miss meetings or scheduled conversations
FREEZE stay still	Absence from work and/or meetings	Avoid or put off decisions	Stay silent in meetings
FLOCK find others	Organize collective responses to feel safe about not speaking alone	Talk behind closed doors	If you can't find people to agree with me within this organization, talking about it with people from other organizations who will join me in my views

Interestingly, it's often the less obvious reactions that are the most difficult to manage because they are subtle and more open to multiple interpretations. And there are more 'Fs' at play that connect the stress people are experiencing and the way they are behaving:

- Fawn – pretending to agree
- Fib – being untruthful, including about whether or not we are OK or what our views are
- F' Off! – saying/doing extreme things as a form of self-sabotage
- Flooded – with Emotions
- Fatigue – tired/drained; this is an effect, rather than a response, but worth looking out for.

For leaders, there is an opportunity to use threat and stress responses as a way of understanding both why and how people are reacting to an Ending.

From there it is possible to:

- Notice cues in our own behaviour or others' behaviour that they are experiencing this Ending as threatening in some way
- Offer compassion, reassurance and support
- Look for ways to minimize the threats.

Endings can be draining and distracting

Once unattended or poorly handled Endings have been uncovered, our clients soon realize the impact those Endings have made on energy, confidence, sense of belonging, creativity, focus, strategic thinking and wellbeing. Whilst these drains on energy and attention may be hard to measure, they are very real. Potentially even more so for our neurodivergent colleagues. For some, the uncertainty and emotional experiences of an Ending are likely to have been challenging to regulate and navigate. Someone with ADHD, for example, isn't necessarily feeling different Emotions to their colleagues, but they may well be feeling them at greater extremes, and for longer periods of time. They may continue to think about it often, and repeatedly experience the same feelings, even after a great deal of time has passed. They may also mask these feelings and experiences, whilst quietly noticing that they are having a different experience compared to others around them. They might try to fit in with their colleagues, masking how they truly feel, and not sharing what they need. All this requires additional energy being expended in unseen and draining ways. Resolving an unattended Ending can be particularly settling for these colleagues.

> ***Consider:*** *What difference would it make to your organization, or indeed to you, if energy, creativity, confidence and focus were increased?*

Exercise 4: What Endings are occurring?

Let's take some time to start connecting what we are saying to your world.

Grab a notepad, tablet or whatever you find useful for thinking.

Divide the page in two, vertically, with a line down the middle. Label the line 'Today'

You now have two columns. The left column is titled 'Past three months' and the right column is titled 'Next three months'.

> Now simply note all the Endings of any kind that have taken place in your organization, and your professional life, in the past three months in the left column. Then add all those you are expecting in the upcoming three months in the right column.
>
> What are you noticing?
>
> How is that feeling today?

Endings are an opportunity for connection

Acknowledging completions, closures, farewells and the many ways we encounter Endings in an organization creates the opportunity to pause, however briefly, and spend some time in celebration, empathy, support and learning. Endings tend to be thought of as a point of separation, when they are in fact a point of connection and an opportunity to deepen our understanding of ourselves and each other. Perhaps by concentrating more on the Endings within the organization we also make more space for the unseen Endings going on in the background to our colleague's working lives: children leaving home, separations, bereavement, house moves, menopause, and all the shifting and changing we constantly encounter in our lives. As leaders, when we account for these things, and understand when they impact presence, or productivity, we have the opportunity to lead kinder, more connected workplaces.

Taking the later train

When Isobel started looking at her relationships with Endings, she realized quite how much of a Beginnings person she was. She had, like many, loved planning ahead, anticipating the new and opportunities that abound in a new Beginning. She would be the first to run for an 'early train' rather than linger in the moments when a group of any kind was disbanding. She is still like that and has learnt to recognize and live with a richer, deeper set of Emotions that exist in acknowledging the Endings she was experiencing. From this exploration she realized discomfort and connection are two sides of the same coin; to acknowledge the discomfort of an Ending was to honour the shared experience and connection. Balanced like this, it became much easier to do both, look back and look forward. Both are possible and can serve us well.

Do we need more, not fewer, Endings?

It's not in our nature to begin with the Ending in mind. Arguably, a fallout of that is continued unnecessary production and consumption, that with better planning of an Ending could have been avoided. We wonder, if we were more accepting of Endings, and planning better for them, could we lead in a more sustainable way that serves our people and our planet better?

Why we avoid Endings

Successful change brought about by properly attending to the psychological transition allows us to fully begin and say hello to today. By naming and accepting Reality, emotionally working through an Ending, marking Accomplishments and finding closure, we release energy and let go of thoughts that we dwell on and hold us back. We improve relationships. We appreciate ourselves and others. We learn and grow.

Leaders who grow their ability to attend to Endings also grow their ability to hold difficult Emotions, to be the adult in the room and to respect, understand and account for different needs and responses to change.

They become better leaders all round, as well as better at attending to Endings.

However, there are many reasons, on a human and a leadership level, as to why we avoid Endings. Not the least of which is that we are not taught this. We're not taught this at school as part of our human development, and it is a topic largely absent from leadership literature and training. The culture in which you have been raised will also impact your levels of engagement and comfort with Endings. William Bridges, in *Managing Transitions*, is one of the few organizational experts who addresses the need to attend to Endings. He teaches us that all successful change programmes do not start with the outcome, 'but the Ending that you have to make to leave the old situation behind'. He rightly points out that it is not the change people resist, it is the letting go. Crucially, though, we don't hear how as leaders we go about attending to Endings, or support others through them.

Our Four Steps of Ending are the guiderail to help you do that. This book is very much about the how.

Before we turn to the Four Steps, let's look at why it is, given all we have just said, that leaders and organizations don't pay attention to Endings.

Focus on the positives

There is, of course, a place for positivity – an important one. But without acceptance of, space for and attention to the full range of human experience and feelings, this positivity risks becoming false. We still regularly hear that putting a brave face on is far more accepted and valued than its less comfortable counterpart, putting an honest face on it. Organizational cultures that value *not* putting a dampener on things, not killing the mood, smile and 'don't be a downer' mean that Endings aren't acknowledged and attended to. We want ease, we want everyone to be OK, so we more fully mark the happy Endings, and we skim or ignore the tricky ones. It might be that we don't even notice the losses, so unattuned are we to their existence and uncomfortable with their impact.

Research published in the *International Journal of Psychotherapy and Research* into the repressing or covering up of Emotion supports our assertion that the truth, and the Emotion and trickiness that comes with it, might well be challenging, but is worth it for the long-term impact: '[While] facing what one has been trying to avoid can elevate one's sense of distress or emotional arousal in the short term, the benefits are far greater as one gains emotional stability, physical and mental health, and also a wider understanding of oneself and others'.

When we work with clients on airing their truth, and the difficulties they are experiencing, rather than conforming to what can become organizational cultures of false positivity, they invariably express relief. They feel lighter. Trust is built. Possibility is opened up and far from draining energy, it is energizing.

Leaders' capacity to hold Emotion and vulnerability

One of our hypotheses is that Endings are less well acknowledged because to do so requires an emotional response; an ability to hold, listen to and express the full range of human Emotions, including sadness, loss, grief and anger.

> ***Consider:*** *What Emotions swirl around Beginnings? Hope, positivity, excitement, possibility, nerves?*
>
> *What Emotions do you immediately think of in terms of Endings? Sadness, anger, grief, missed opportunity?*

But we are making huge assumptions if we think in this way; let's take care not to take a binary view of Emotions as positive or negative or to see Emotions simplistically as things that are felt one at a time. Humans are complex. We can be relieved, sad and excited simultaneously. By discounting the need to acknowledge an Ending, we miss the opportunity to both name how we are feeling and celebrate what was contributed and appreciated. When all Emotions are welcome, more becomes possible.

It takes emotional self-regulation and maturity to sit with the discomfort of loss, knowing that in an Ending there will be disappointment, guilt or unfulfilled possibilities. In the world of Endings, Emotions can run high, and we have observed them running even higher as a direct consequence of leaders ignoring them; conversations may then happen behind closed doors, leaving people feeling unheard or without an opportunity to be honest about how they feel. Eventually this may lead to an increased emotional response. A leader who understands that an Ending is a part of the future makes what comes next more likely to succeed.

Much of this is about Emotions and pace. In this data driven, rational world of work, navigating and making time for strong negative Emotions to be allowed, acknowledged and felt can be a scary place for leaders to go – for themselves, and in support of the organization they lead.

Emotion, as we repeatedly say, is at the heart of the work. So much about Endings and Good Byes is about Emotions: the fear-based ones, such as disappointment, resentment or regret; and the love-based ones, like belonging, feeling part of a team, empathy or loyalty. In avoiding fear or negative-based Emotions, we deny a full acknowledgement of the energizing positive ones.

For example, anger is a useful Emotion; felt at its purest, it shows a boundary has been breached. Anger is healthy and normal. However, many of us have internalized a sense, or maybe a belief, that feeling or expressing anger is not OK. So, it either doesn't come out, or it finds its way out, for example in a passive aggressive avoidant way, or in a pseudo polite way: 'I am a little bit frustrated'. When we allow anger to be processed properly and worked through our system it can be released and we can all move on. All Emotion is a response to some stimulus, as Megan Devine says in *It's OK That You're Not OK*, 'shushed anger joins a backlog of disallowed emotions, popping up in health issues, interpersonal challenges and mental torment'.

Facing in to loss

Endings, and our relationship to them, goes deep. It is about belonging (a basic human need) and loss. Loss is subjective, utterly individual and yet so often is simultaneously part of a collective experience that adds further layers of meaning and complexity. As leaders we can't assume that if we have moved on, that others have too.

Loss is more complex, more subtle and more interwoven than people sometimes think and there are many, many types of loss happening every day in our organizations. Losses of independence, access, purpose, direction, intended outcome, results, friendship, sense of self, time, familiarity and more.

As Megan Devine says, 'When we start talking about loss, it's like this sudden permission… We all carry stories that need acknowledgement'.

π In *The Inner Work of Age*, Connie Zweig explores the transition into the later chapter in life, when we have the opportunity to return to or discover what ignites us outside of our work. She explores what might be possible when we move beyond economic activity. In our experience of working with leaders, there is often an assumption that getting to a stage in life where one of our life's key motivators – that of working to reach our economic goals – has been achieved, will be an overwhelmingly positive experience. The Reality is often far more uncomfortable than that.

Who am I now?
We worked with a very successful Sales Director, Björn, whose Long-Term Incentive Plan was secured, he and his children wanting for nothing. What a fortunate place to be in you would think. He was in his early 50s, and wanted to carry on being purposeful, productive and doing what he did best. He was deeply troubled by needing to redirect this energy and dive into the unknown. He realized that his sense of

his own value was entirely caught up in the identity and success of the organization, and that 'value' was making money for the organization, and making money for himself and his family. After six months of exploration with us, Björn had a useful way forward. He started a consultancy to keep feeding his need to work, became a Trustee of a local charity and became an assistant coach for his daughter's football team (for which he had no qualification, and therefore went on a steep learning curve of not being in charge!) What was coming to an end was the sense of his identity that was wrapped up in work, his need to be in charge and his drive for money. What began was a refreshing new chapter where he learnt new skills, and humility; he redirected the huge amount of energy and vigour he latterly used to 'hitting his targets' into something different.

Fix and rescue

What also stops leaders attending well to Endings is the leadership trap of needing to fix and rescue. For example, faced with the disappointment of a project team disbanded due to new strategic priorities, it's hard to listen to and acknowledge disappointment, and missed opportunities, without wanting to smooth, fix and move on to easier, less painful or awkward territory. The pain means that often Endings are dealt with too quickly, or with a focus on process – sort this, get it done and get it over with so we can all move on. The ripping off of the sticking plaster is the trade off we make for a more intense pain that is soon forgotten. Unlike the plaster though, the pain lingers for people involved in Endings that haven't been properly attended to, and then we have two very different approaches in the mix – 'hurry up, look away and move on' and 'slow down, look at me, this hurts' are uncomfortable bedfellows.

When we expect people to minimize the impact of socially painful circumstances, and when we ignore them and expect others to ignore them too, we not only quite literally inflict pain, but we are also actually being counterproductive. These actions leave people feeling hurt and resisting more.

Feeling betrayed

One of the first examples we shared with you in our introduction was the experience of someone leaving a team or organization where those left behind felt betrayed. This is so common – to feel that in leaving, someone has let you down. It feels personal. Whether it's a graduate who after six months realizes this isn't for them, or a CEO who leaves just as the signs on the horizon are that all is not well, those left behind lose their perspective that people have a right to make choices and decisions about what is best for them. Perhaps those left behind secretly wish they could or would leave too. Or perhaps this leader had supported them and invested in their development, or they simply really loved working with this person.

The resulting behaviour means that the full Reality isn't acknowledged, including people's right to choose to leave. Feelings of betrayal are the dominant Emotion and often, as a result, Accomplishments and Ritual are not fully attended to.

What we're highlighting here is a confusion that often arises between being loyal and not leaving. Leaving is viewed as disloyal. In fact, leaving is leaving. It might be that there are important and legitimate conversations expressing disappointment or concern that someone is leaving; there may be a sense of unfairness acknowledged, or investment in someone having been essentially 'wasted'. Working through that messy Reality is about finding ways to express and work through it, rather than getting stuck in a sense of injustice and betrayal that can lead to unkind treatment of the person that is leaving.

How dare you

Maddy made a career choice she thought was going to be for life. It was a vocation, within a public service organization that many employees served in for life. The nature of the work relies heavily on close knit teams and working relationships that are about togetherness and having each other's backs.

Maddy embarked on this career (and at this point she believed it would be her lifelong career and was fully committed to that) full of excitement about what she would be learning and becoming and full of hope of how she was going to be of service.

The Reality that became apparent through her first year was that she didn't enjoy the work. It surprised and unsettled her that the role didn't use her skills in a way she imagined. Alongside this ran her experience of this being a hierarchical ranked organization in which she didn't fully feel she could be her best self. She didn't feel she belonged.

After two years Maddy took the brave decision to leave and pursue another career.

The system which demanded loyalty, and was under pressure and under resourced, reacted with frustration and anger. They were initially unable to see the human experience beneath their sense of disappointment and betrayal. Despite being treated differently (and badly), Maddy continued to work hard right up to her last day. In doing so she won back some hearts and minds and there was some recognition not only of the great contribution she had made in a short time, but perhaps of the responsibility they shared for her experience.

Had the organization done the work of naming the Reality, acknowledging and clearing the Emotions and moving through Accomplishments and Ritual then perhaps the energy could have been more quickly and productively turned to lessons learned.

Consider: *Why was it that Maddy left? How might they retain the next person for longer?*

In circumstances like these, where the leaders exercise emotional maturity and acknowledge what worked and what needed work on all sides, not only does the person that leaves have a better experience, but those people left behind feel better too. If it isn't attended to, the feeling of betrayal will linger and potentially be felt by others who had nothing to do with it, and that energy could be better used elsewhere.

Ghosts and entanglements

Data from The Decelerator helpline[4] tells us that approximately 75% of calls reference feelings or experiences that callers associate with past events or losses, both within and beyond organizational contexts. Mismanaged or avoided Endings leave their mark. Leaders are often carrying their own Endings baggage, which means that they may be triggered by an Ending they are dealing with in the present, resulting in the past flooding back in. Before they know it, they are in their own stuff instead of being present for those they lead.

Here's an example of a leader that was entangled by their own ghosts.

Still haunted

Anisa had been a whistle blower in her previous organization, and subsequently been victimized, leading to her being exited abruptly with a compromise agreement. As a result of her bruising experience she had become hypersensitive to how people feel. In her current role, she had an underperforming staff member who she had been doing everything within her power to support. It became the necessary and appropriate thing for Anisa to let this person go. Repeatedly, she got to the point of having that conversation, but found a reason to avoid it. Anisa came to us to work on this. We noticed, and shared with Anisa, that we

---

[4] The Decelerator helpline supports organizations in the charity sector to plan for closing, and closing well.

> *kept hearing her talk about her past experience of leaving after whistleblowing and how much that had affected her, rather than working through her current challenges. Anisa realized that the treatment she had received was getting in the way of managing Endings for others. She kept getting stuck in the full-colour version of her own Ending. We worked through the REAR Steps (Reality, Emotions, Accomplishments and Ritual – that we will explore in detail through the rest of this book) with Anisa to help her understand how it was impacting her decision-making in the present, and the leader she wanted to be in relation to her values and how she treated people, especially at the point of exit. Anisa was then able to use the REAR Steps to preview and plan a thoughtful, compassionate and clear exit for the individual.*

As Anisa's story demonstrates, when unattended, Endings leave scars and ghosts. Those ghosts, when acknowledged and worked through, can become the foundation for the values and behaviours that make for a better leader of Endings.

Why we avoid Endings – the organizational lens

Process gets in the way

Even when a leader is willing to acknowledge an Ending and work through discomfort in order to do so, they will often then find these intentions thwarted by organizational structures and processes. Whilst these processes are designed to protect both the individuals and the integrity of the organization, even when done with care, what they often have are unforeseen and damaging consequences.

A fear of backlash can sometimes mean the leader is encouraged not to acknowledge a loss. The fear of undermining a process such as a compromise agreement[5] or of saying the wrong thing amid a complex set of secrets that are being kept can be daunting and lead to paralysis.

Compromise agreements are commonplace and often necessary. However, compromise agreements, by definition, silence some people and create secrets. Details of settlements and reasons for leaving may need to be legally kept secret.

The systemic consequences ripple out into the culture and are held as baggage elsewhere in the organization. It may show up as gossip, mistrust, lethargy or resistance. Any number of compromise agreements doesn't stop the wider system feeling and absorbing the affects.

Pace

Organizational fast pace and processes get in the way.

Leaders are under ever-increasing pressure to perform. Nothing stays still or constant. There is churn, Beginnings

---

[5] A compromise agreement is a legal contract where an employee receives compensation upon leaving an organization in exchange for waiving the right to pursue further legal claims. It also often involves non-disclosure agreements where the parties are not then able to talk about their experiences, including why the employment has come to an end.

and Endings occurring all the time. This is the Reality and context within which leaders operate and it is never more the case than now.

The following example of organizational pace refers to our experience of leaders and their organization during the Covid-19 pandemic. We want to be clear, as we have mentioned before, that this book is about organizational Endings; it is not offering guidance for dealing with the death of a colleague. For that we suggest you seek specialist grief and loss support. We say this from a place of deep compassion for all those who have lost a loved one or a colleague in this time, and also from a place of care of knowing the boundary and scope of the application of our work.

In our experience, the Global Pandemic increased the pace and intensity of work and some of the habits formed in those urgent times have stuck. As we went through successive lockdowns, there was rapid change and so much had to be done differently. But because of the urgency and the extremely challenging context, there wasn't time to pause. That pace has then become the habit for many.

For example, when many of us pivoted to online meetings, the questionable practice of 'back to back meetings' was escalated. For many leaders and organizations who have not taken stock, paused and looked at ways of working, this culture of continuous meetings has prevailed.

When pace leads to a lack of care and attention to detail, it can also lead to monumental consequences.

🪱 *Sweat the small stuff*

Elif worked in a team which covered Europe, Middle East and Africa (EMEA). She was based in Istanbul, and her line manager was in Milan. Her line manager's personal assistant contacted her via email to say that he wanted to come and have a face-to-face meeting with Elif. This was out of the normal rhythm of their interactions. When the manager sent a meeting invitation to Elif it was titled 'Elif/Luca redundancy notice'.

You can imagine the 48 hours Elif had awaiting that meeting; it did not go well for either party.

So much ended in the Covid-19 pandemic, without time to acknowledge and pause. Particularly stark was the number of important Rituals that had to be missed because we weren't able to gather in groups. Schools, which have traditionally been really good at marking Endings to help young people transition to new Beginnings, were unable to complete their usual Rituals. Proms (as a mark of the end of secondary school), award ceremonies and sports days were all cancelled. As time went on, versions of these Rituals were taking place online, as educators instinctively knew their importance in transition. Later we saw that, where possible, ceremonies which had been cancelled were held in subsequent years. Many universities held additional graduation ceremonies for cohorts who had missed theirs.

Consider: *What could the corporate world learn from this?*

We all tend to rush to appealing Beginnings, and what leaders may experience in terms of resistance may well be because of that hurry and people not having taken the opportunity to acknowledge the loss. Another consequence of moving at speed is the lack of succession planning and preparation both to leave and to begin.

Rabbi Joseph Dweck, speaking at a debate hosted by the Windsor Leadership Trust, explained why a slower pace in his transition from his previous role in New York to that of a Senior Rabbi position in the UK was needed:

> *It comes with the responsibility of leadership to succession plan, and think about who comes next, and how you leave the environment they will inhabit. When I got my new job I asked for a year [to transition], so that I could work on how I left the place I was leaving, in order to truly begin where I was going.*
>
> Rabbi Joseph Dweck, Windsor Leadership Debate, September 2019

Another impact of pace is how many Endings there are as a result. The impact of small cumulative stresses over time is a loss of resilience, and ultimately can mean that for some, the dam breaks.

The Reality is that Endings, pain and loss will feature in your life and in the life of your organization. This is as true of perceived positive transitions, such as a promotion, as any other kind of Ending. Left unattended, these Endings have an impact.

> *Do not go where the path may lead, go instead where there is no path and leave a trail.*
>
> Ralph Waldo Emerson

We need to learn how to navigate Endings as part of our working lives.

When leaders mishandle or ignore Endings, the impact ripples out and ripples on. There is often a connection to their own history with Endings and the scars they have left. This is the reason why we say start with yourselves as leaders. In Chapter 3 you'll find a more detailed explanation of why as a leader, you need to go first, and in Chapter 4 we offer some questions that will help you to work through your own experiences.

> ***Consider:*** *What are you doing to prepare yourself to lead with presence, compassion and confidence through Endings?*

Our Four Steps of Ending will offer you, as a leader, a guiderail for navigating Endings for yourself and in support of others, both individually and collectively. Next, we'll share with you what those Four Steps are, and then how to go about using them in your life as a leader.

Looking back to look forward

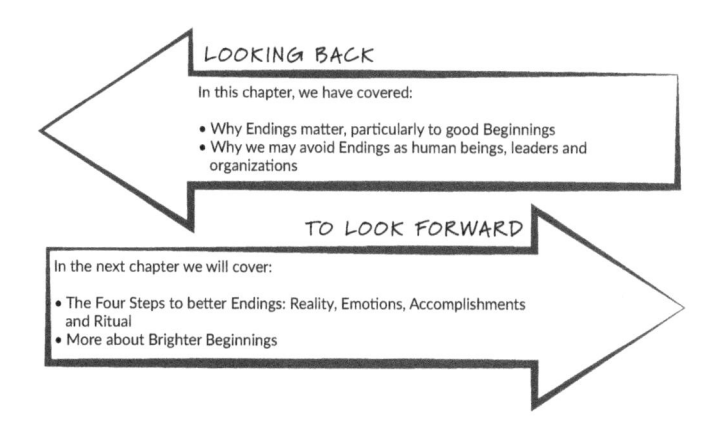

LOOKING BACK

In this chapter, we have covered:

- Why Endings matter, particularly to good Beginnings
- Why we may avoid Endings as human beings, leaders and organizations

TO LOOK FORWARD

In the next chapter we will cover:

- The Four Steps to better Endings: Reality, Emotions, Accomplishments and Ritual
- More about Brighter Beginnings

REAR

- RITUAL
- ACCOMPLISHMENTS
- EMOTIONS
- REALITY

Chapter 2

The Four Steps – An introduction to REAR

It matters a great deal to us that the leaders we work with leave us with an understanding of how to actively apply the insights they have gained through their work with us.

Our work has led us to create a Four Step model for navigating Endings in organizations.

The model is simple – we find that the most useful application arises when thinking has expanded and been given depth and breadth, and then is distilled back into simple, useful, applicable Steps. From there it's about using those Steps usefully by applying them to your world and the things that are happening in it.

During one of our workshops a leader described our model as 'a guiderail that steadied them and guided them across the slippery floor of Endings'. The 'how to' piece is coming in the following chapters. First, let's take you through our guiderail, organized into Four Steps.

This model is easy to remember too, not least because if you have identified an Ending, you could pay more attention to your REAR:

REAR

1. Reality (naming it – including the tricky and messy stuff)
2. Emotions (the heart of the work, recognizing and allowing for these)
3. Accomplishments (seeing what can be celebrated before, during and after the Ending – there is always something)
4. Ritual (stems from the first Four Steps, to close, with or without words)

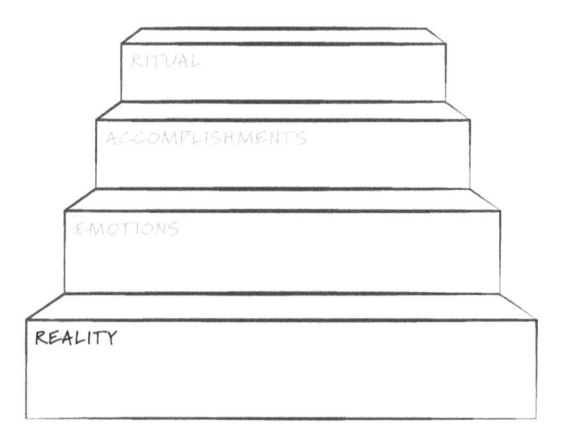

RITUAL
ACCOMPLISHMENTS
EMOTIONS
REALITY

Step 1: REALITY

We are dangerous when we are not conscious of our responsibility for how we behave, think and feel.
Marshall B. Rosenberg

Let's start with Reality – naming the Ending, including the messy stuff! We will fully name what is coming to an end and the complete Reality of it, including both gains and losses. This is about adding the detail and taking responsibility as a leader. So, for example, when somebody is leaving, truly and fully acknowledge all the ways that it will be different both in practical and emotional terms. A beautifully simple question, that when it is fully answered reveals layers and layers of practical and emotional Reality, is *'How will Monday be different?'* Or as a project closes, naming the time taken, the investment, the people that have worked on it, the results, the impact and more.

The Reality is often more complex than leaders give it credit for. It needs us to pause and separate out and name its different elements. It sounds obvious, but it's the bit that is so easily skipped or rushed because the assumption we make is that because something is on our minds we have really acknowledged it to be true. It is the difference between intellectually knowing something, and really knowing something emotionally. This first Step can sometimes hit you like a thunderbolt.

If we don't untangle the Reality, it can entangle us. This is what we mean by tricky and messy stuff.

When something comes to an end it might have been successful or unsuccessful, the people involved may or may not have had choice and agency in the decision. It might have happened on time and is expected, or happened out of the blue for those on the receiving end. There is often messy stuff involved in bringing something to a close, on the leaders' part and for those affected. Often, this messy stuff can't be talked about openly and publicly. This can, in turn, lead to an assumption that the best thing to do is say little and move on quickly, in case it raises awkward moments or questions. Messy stuff often has conflicting elements to it and is closely linked to the second Step of this work, Emotions.

Some examples we have encountered with our clients as messy stuff could be:

> We will have a compromise agreement, therefore what can I truly say and express?

> It wasn't my choice to close the department, but I am accountable for leading the process.

> I am secretly relieved that she has taken voluntary redundancy, otherwise I would need to look for head count savings elsewhere.

> She used to be my boss and brought me into this organization. She has been exited after a recent re-structure. I am being promoted. I wouldn't be here if it wasn't for her.

In naming the Reality, including the messy stuff, we also begin to deepen our understanding of who and what is affected.

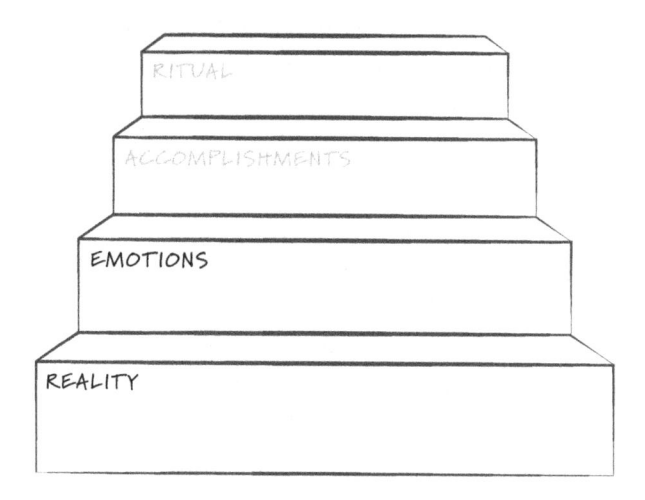

Step 2: EMOTIONS

All learning has an emotional base.

Plato

We've arrived at Step 2, Emotions – quite literally the heart of the work. This work is most usefully done after you have attended to Step 1, Reality, including the messy stuff.

The Reality is that pain and loss will feature in your life and in the life of your organization. As human beings we don't often attend fully to the Endings we are experiencing. We don't face the Reality that everything and everyone has a finite life. It is an uncomfortable truth.

Listening to our clients, it is often avoiding the difficult and emotional conversations, as a result of a wish to avoid pain, conflict, anger, regret and sadness, that leads us to shield our emotional selves. In closing down that emotional Reality of loss we can miss the opportunity to look at the other side of the emotional coin where we find love, belonging, gratitude and joy. Paying more attention to the Emotions Step can grow our ability to stand in our own difficulties.

The role of Emotion in leadership has been given an increasingly welcome place at the table. Thanks to the work of researchers like Susan David and Brené Brown, vulnerability, trust and empathy are increasingly desirable qualities and skills in the workplace. And yet, the reality in our experience is more of an emphasis on tempering Emotions, particularly 'negative' ones, in order that they don't get in the way of pace and progress.

For the many reasons we have explored in this book, it can be daunting for leaders to make space for strong Emotions, both for themselves and in support of their organization. Emotions are rarely neat or singular; they often come in complex combinations, which we can be unaware of. As Aristotle said, 'Anyone can become angry – that is easy. But to be angry with the right person, to the right degree, at the right time, for the right purpose and in the right way – that is not easy'.

Putting ourselves in a position to be able to accept and acknowledge the greater emotional complexity of an Ending opens up so many more possibilities.

Imagine the impact of the leader who doesn't shy away from the fact that both Beginnings and Endings are everywhere – a leader who understands that an Ending is a part of the future and makes what comes next possible. Rather than suppressing the Emotion of an Ending, we have gone towards it, and now we can do the work of acknowledgement through the Accomplishments Step.

```
        ┌─────────────────┐
        │     RITUAL      │
    ┌───┴─────────────────┴───┐
    │     ACCOMPLISHMENTS     │
┌───┴─────────────────────────┴───┐
│           EMOTIONS              │
┌┴─────────────────────────────────┴┐
│             REALITY               │
└───────────────────────────────────┘
```

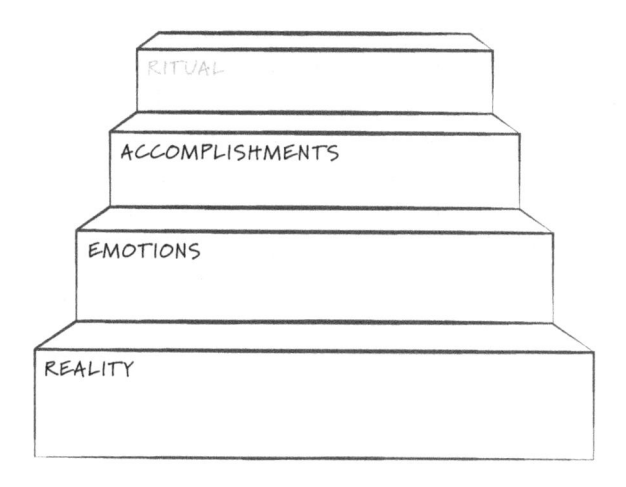

Step 3: ACCOMPLISHMENTS

Change takes place best in a large context of genuine praise.

Nancy Kline

We're now at Step 3, Accomplishments. This work is most usefully done after you have attended to Step 1, Reality, including the messy stuff, and Step 2, Emotions.

This Step is about the sense of completion that comes when what has been accomplished is acknowledged. It's a Step that tends to get attention when things have gone well and gets difficult when things are messy. It's also one that can have long-lasting consequences for individuals and teams trying to focus on the present and future but finding themselves repeatedly lost in thoughts and feelings that their contribution has not been recognized. It is essentially about being seen and being heard.

When an Ending has gone well – such as the completion of a successful project or pitch, or someone being promoted into a role having been successful where they were – it's probably safe to say that the Accomplishments Step gets some automatic attention in the form of what's essentially a 'well done' and 'thank you'. Does it necessarily happen well though? This Step can often be rushed even when we're celebrating. We feel pretty certain we know what has been accomplished and end up skipping ahead to Ritual without truly giving this thought.

Here is an example.

Making thank you meaningful

A team didn't feel that their Accomplishments and contributions to a successful year were recognized and appreciated. The leader could point to scripts and meeting notes where they had said 'thank you' many times. We worked with the leader to pause and more thoughtfully close the year. By being specific and descriptive, linking to the company's mission and values, she illustrated the impact they had had, and why it was important. It transformed how her colleagues felt seen and heard and their Accomplishments truly appreciated.

And what about when things have gone badly? Poor results or complicated confidentiality agreements when someone leaves, for example. The consequences of tricky and messy stuff can be a lack of acknowledgement of Accomplishment. Leaving without a sense of Accomplishment has an impact on the individual, on those who have witnessed someone leave in that way and on the organizations that are being left and joined. Identifying Accomplishments is also a key preparation for the Ritual that acknowledges the end of something, and fully makes way for the Beginning.

With Endings rarely being tied up in a neat bow, exactly as we imagined they would be at the Beginning, we can easily (and often do) miss the Step of acknowledging all that came to pass, all we learned, and all that we accomplished. Sometimes, the journey from exhilaration and celebration of the end of a project to anxiety about how it's going to land can be short and fast. So fast, that people might lack the confidence to celebrate something that would still be subject to feedback and end up not celebrating it at all. Once leaders start spotting missed opportunities to celebrate, the list grows fast.

There is always something accomplished, and always a way, even if you never actually say it directly to that person, to be truthful about what has been accomplished. And if you are someone who was part of an Ending where Accomplishments weren't acknowledged, and it's still on your mind, this is work you can choose to do for yourself.

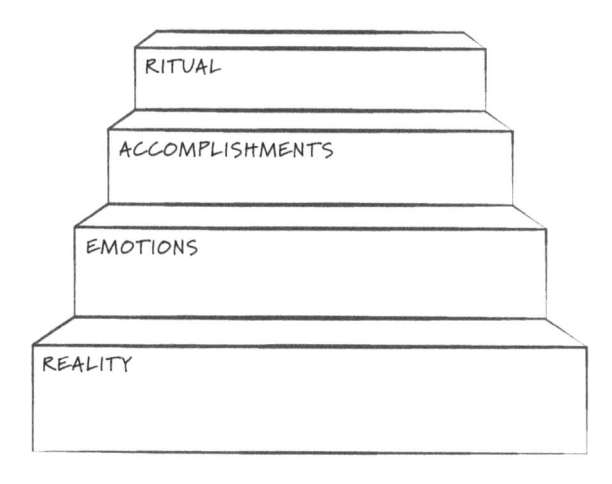

```
                    ┌─────────────────┐
                    │ RITUAL          │
            ┌───────┴─────────────────┴───────┐
            │ ACCOMPLISHMENTS                 │
    ┌───────┴─────────────────────────────────┴───────┐
    │ EMOTIONS                                        │
┌───┴─────────────────────────────────────────────────┴───┐
│ REALITY                                                 │
└─────────────────────────────────────────────────────────┘
```

Step 4: RITUAL

Ceremony creates change and is transformative in itself, whilst supporting a sense of great ease as we experience the transitions of life.

Sandra Ingerman

A Ritual is an activity or a series of actions in a recognized, predictable and suitable order. A Ritual can be elaborate and complex, and can also be a quiet, simple acknowledgement. It might be that you think of religious ceremony, which it can be, but it can also be the regular practice of, for example, taking five minutes with your morning coffee to listen to the birdsong and read a newspaper. It can be a performance or a ceremony of some kind, which is often enacted more through Emotion and thought or intellectual interaction. The most ancient Ritual we know, across all faiths and cultures, is the Ritual of the ultimate Good Bye, in the death of a loved one. These Rituals have been created to give us a sense of safety and structure around how we do that and support us in moving into a future without that person.

Rituals come in many forms, from events to celebrating mergers or completed projects, or the leaving 'do', or the making of a speech or a ceremony to present an award or gift. Schools do it well for their students, offering their young people yearbooks, graduation or prize giving ceremonies, proms, T-shirts with all the class names. The military does this well by acknowledging Endings with Rituals such as retirement ceremonies, change of command ceremonies and farewell salutes, which honour service, recognize contributions and mark transitions. The Rituals we tend to be most familiar with at work are the leaving speeches, the retirement parties, the leaving card signed by everybody, the presentation of a gift or the celebration drinks. We also see a form of Ritual in many foyers, where the history of the organization is celebrated, and people or products that have been important through its history are added to the walls, and awards are displayed.

Rituals can be used in organizations to acknowledge feelings, loss and give an unspoken place for difficult Emotions such as guilt. They celebrate what has been, and equally offer a place to celebrate and acknowledge what will be next. Here are some examples of Ritual done well.

Mugs and moustaches

A mug was produced for everyone post-merger who went on into the new organization, and said, 'we survived the cull'. In that collective gift and brief phrase an Emotion was captured and acknowledged with wry humour.

***

If you are ever in the UK and pass through Twyford railway station you'll see the portrait of the station master, Norman Topsom. Norman first started working at the station in 1964, until his retirement in 2015. He was known for his happy disposition, dedication to the upkeep of the station and trademark whiskers and handlebar moustache! When he retired from this dedicated service at a surprise ceremony, he was invited to unveil his portrait that will forever remain on Platform 4, as well as having a train named after him.

🕸 *Timely tidying*

The All Blacks men's rugby team has a Ritual called Sweeping the Shed. In his book, Legacy, James Kerr describes how after every match, regardless of their location, the All Blacks team gathers to tidy up their locker room. This practice promotes humility, gratitude and the principle that all team members are equal.

We see Ritual in the theatre too. Often, at the end of a performance the crew are dismantling the set, actors and directors are in conversation with audience members, costumes are being put away – everyone is busy with jobs that need to be done, rather than a shared moment of reflection and appreciation.

🕸 *The final curtain*

We know of a drama society that has a Ritual after a final performance. The following day everyone (so not only stage crew, but everyone also involved) gets together to dismantle the set as the signal that they are closing this world that they have temporarily created together. While they do so, they talk about the realities (the highs and lows of rehearsals and performances), the Emotions and the achievements. In this example, the first three Steps form part of the fourth – the Ritual is the container for the reflections.

As you can see, there are many ways we can use everything we have learned from the first three Steps to say a proper Good Bye to something in the form of a Ritual of some kind. In doing so we are able to turn our energy and attention more fully to the future because the Accomplishments, facts and Emotions have been given their rightful place.

And as with the Accomplishments Step, if you are not able to do this work now, or even if years have passed since the opportunity for the Ritual was missed, it is still work you can choose to quietly do yourself that will have an impact.

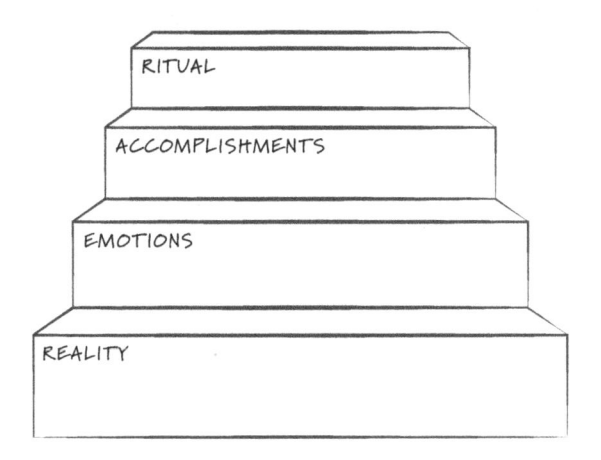

```
        ┌─────────────────┐
        │ RITUAL          │
    ┌───┴─────────────────┴────────┐
    │ ACCOMPLISHMENTS              │
┌───┴──────────────────────────────┴────┐
│ EMOTIONS                              │
├───────────────────────────────────────┴────┐
│ REALITY                                    │
└────────────────────────────────────────────┘
```

Brighter Beginnings

Working through the Four Steps brings multiple benefits to individuals, teams and organizations. Trust builds, along with confidence, courage, empathy, energy and focus.

Endings work is not just nice to have, it's about organizational health and performance.

Now whenever we have a client in transition or leading change, we invite them to start with orientating towards the Ending they may be ignoring. Every time, our experience is that once they have attended to the Four Steps of the Ending, they acknowledge what they want to take with them from the past situation, and what they want to respectfully leave behind. There is a moment of real focus where the discretionary energy that is bound up in the past is released, and they fully orientate themselves to the present and future.

Exercise 5: The value of attending to Endings

Think back to the list of Endings you made on page 31.

Imagine if all those Endings were navigated in a way that released energy, focus, creativity and confidence, and strengthened team relationships and communication.
- What would that be worth to your organization?

The importance of the order

In our workshops a question that often gets asked is 'does the order matter?'

The simple answer is yes. Each Step of REAR is enriched by the one before it, and starting with acknowledging Reality and closing with Ritual is a process that then feels complete. It's OK to loop back round to Reality and Emotions many times over, covering many different aspects of the Ending as you notice and uncover them, before moving on to Accomplishments and Ritual.

Rushed re-structuring

> Let's look at the example of a manager, Priya, who has avoided having performance conversations with a direct report (Rohan) who is struggling. When a restructure of the team presents an opportunity to let Rohan go, Priya takes it with open arms. In

acknowledging one feeling – the relief and rushing towards not having to manage the individual anymore – Priya fast forwards to letting them go. The Ritual at this point is more about how Priya feels than how Rohan feels, and it is hurried and superficial. Priya fails to acknowledge Rohan's past Accomplishments, their relationship and the many feelings that are swirling around. If Priya worked through their own REAR Steps it could be very different:

Reality: *Rohan has been underperforming for 18 months. Coaching and performance conversations have been offered and feedback has been given. Priya was considering letting them go. The restructure is an opportunity to do that.*

Emotions: *Priya is feeling guilty at their avoidance and culpability, relief in being rid of the responsibility and prospect of needing to deal with Rohan's underperformance, and sad as they were once friends and peers. Further work would no doubt reveal more tricky and messy stuff, together with the opportunity to loop round Reality and Emotion until there is a full picture.*

Accomplishments: *having been able to work through their own entanglements and Emotions, Priya is able to acknowledge the contribution Rohan has made, including remembering what they saw in them at the point of hire. Priya then gathers examples of stories and deliverables from better times. This also enables the acknowledgment of the strengths that Rohan will take to their next role.*

> **Ritual:** Priya writes a very personal card acknowledging all of the above and gives it to Rohan over a closing coffee.

It may be that you uncover or are reminded of an Ending in the past that wasn't attended to. This work makes it possible to re-visit those. It is never too late to acknowledge an Ending and in doing so to have a positive impact on the future that has been affected by that Ending. It may be that you need several Rituals. Your understanding of the Four Steps will inform the Rituals that the system, and the teams and individuals within it, most need. So, for any Ritual to fully serve its purpose of making way for a new Beginning, it needs the support of the first three Steps. Each Step is informed and strengthened by the previous one.

The example of the impact of missing Steps we hear most often is that of the profound and lasting impact it has on an individual when they exit a team or organization and there is a Ritual that they find insincere or inappropriate. Shadows are cast and there is long-lasting impact when a person leaves without feeling seen or heard. And that impact is felt by the person leaving, and all the witnesses to it.

We'll explore this idea further as we move on to how you can now apply the Steps to the Endings in your organization. We are aware as we offer this that this is an area that people often choose not to go towards for the very reasons that we wrote the original article. While there is work to do to release energy, restore or embed pride, create a sense of strength and build relationships, this process can also be painful, challenging and emotive and can be a bit messy. This is why we created the guiderail. We encourage you to leave time and space for this work, to pace yourself, to seek support if you need it and as you'll see as you read on, that it's best to start with yourself.

Looking back to look forward

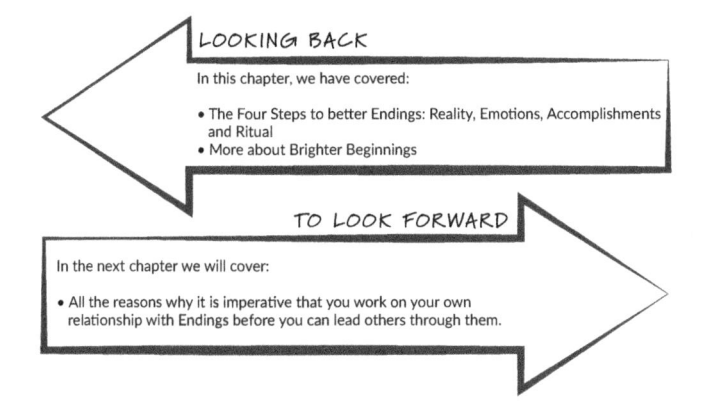

LOOKING BACK

In this chapter, we have covered:

- The Four Steps to better Endings: Reality, Emotions, Accomplishments and Ritual
- More about Brighter Beginnings

TO LOOK FORWARD

In the next chapter we will cover:

- All the reasons why it is imperative that you work on your own relationship with Endings before you can lead others through them.

Chapter 3

You go first

Our own history of Good Byes will affect how we as leaders acknowledge and attend to Endings in our organizations, and our capacity to hold and facilitate a Good Bye for those we lead. In *Still Moving*, Deborah Rowland highlights that 'The dual capacity to be aware of, and able to regulate our response to, experience guides the entire quality of our thinking, action and results.' It is important not to underestimate the skill and depth of understanding both required by and impacted by this work. Endings work intercepts several crucial areas of leadership:

- **Leading Change:** in this permacrisis world, leaders are pivoting their businesses constantly. This has an impact on the human capital, many of whom may be change weary or resistant.
- **Emotional Agility:** being able to understand, manage and regulate your Emotions and be present and attentive to the Emotions of those you lead.
- **Navigating Loss and Grief:** it is not just the ultimate Good Bye – death that brings up loss and grief. It is also loss of a sense of belonging, loss of opportunity or loss of status. Grief and loss are complex, therefore you need to feel grounded and OK yourself.

- **Systemic Thinking:** when we think systemically, we include those who came before and those who came after. There is an impact on those who stay, and those who are left behind. An expression we use with leaders (taken from the Charles Dickens' book of the same name) is Christmas Carol thinking. In other words, considering the ghosts of the past, present and future.
- **Self-Awareness:** the more aware a leader is of themselves, their views, preferences, strengths and potential blind spots, the more they are enabling themselves to be flexible, curious, consistent and confident. It is rare that we talk with a leader who has spent time on their relationship with Endings before we discuss it with them, and it is therefore an opportunity to significantly grow their self-awareness.
- **Psychological Safety:** a self-aware, reflective, empathetic leader is better equipped to build trust and a sense of security.
- **Strategic Thinking:** paying attention to Endings enriches the awareness of learning from the past and strengthens strategic thinking and decision-making. Looking at Endings does not keep you stuck in the past – far from it. In fact, it releases energy and creativity and the sense of possibility for the future because the past has been fully understood and acknowledged.

It is this very complexity that makes this chapter about you, the most important chapter. Why? Because in our experience as practitioners, trainers, coaches and people who have been through a lot of self-development, we know one key thing to be true. You have to do your own work first. If you are reading this book in the hope of picking up handy ways to support others through Endings then great, you will get that. However, unless you stop, reflect and think about your own Endings, and your patterns, and your own relationship to Endings, your leadership in relation to Endings risks being hollow, inauthentic and ultimately less impactful. You will risk getting tripped up by something in your own relationship with Endings, or missing the opportunity to acknowledge something that is important to your teams and your organization because it had been a blind spot for you.

We have witnessed how other shifts in organizational culture, like Diversity and Inclusion work, or coaching cultures, grow well and sustainably when they are in the hands of people that start with themselves and take full responsibility for their ongoing learning. The additional benefit of starting with yourself is being clearer on what you feel able and confident to hold as a leader, and what you will need additional support for.

Other reasons to start by better understanding yourself in relation to Endings (in order to be better equipped to lead through Endings) include the following points.

Emotional awareness and literacy

When we shy away, brush over or even ignore Endings, we are denying our true range of emotional possibilities. This is beautifully illustrated by the Pixar film *Inside Out*. A little girl and her parents move away from her friends and home to start over. She is overcome with sadness and anger, and the joyous little girl her parents love and praise has been hidden. Through the brilliant narrative of seeing the five basic Emotions of joy, sadness, anger, fear and disgust that run her mind, played out as animated characters inside her head, we see how when sadness and anger are given space, more is possible.

That is why we believe this work is so closely aligned and builds on Emotional Intelligence (Daniel Goleman) and Emotional Agility (Susan David). Our framework gently guides you through expanding your emotional awareness, increasing your emotional lexicon. This might be challenging for you, depending on how you experience your Emotions, what you allow to be present, what you avoid or deny space for. That is why it is critical to start with yourself, so you can learn and then be more available to those who you lead.

Identity

Some Endings, by definition, are very personal and focused on an individual. Redundancy and retirement are good examples of how leaving can have a deep impact, leading to a questioning of their sense of identity. For example, we have seen retiring leaders struggle with a sense of who they are, and where the loss of status, purpose and structure can lead to an existential struggle of 'who am I outside of this building?'

This is what one of our clients said in a session exploring retirement.

What do you do?

He had completed lifelong service in a large institution and had dedicated not only most of his working life, but also much of his family life to the organization. He found it hard to imagine who he was or could be as he emerged and entered retirement. In working with him on this Ending, it revealed that the fear of going forward was too great to face it.

Who am I, if I'm not this? How can I possibly answer the question that gets asked every time you meet someone new, 'What do you do?'

As a leader, knowing yourself and considering how you would feel in these situations is the gateway to empathy and being able to support others through their Endings at work.

Different starting and Ending points

You may be starting from a different position in relation to the Ending. As a leader, you may be the architect of the Ending, either consciously or unconsciously. For example, if you have restructured your department, there will be a number of Endings and Beginnings. You will know some of what is going to happen before others do. You will have awareness of the possible consequences before those who it impacts. You may well have more agency over the events than those impacted by them. You may be directly affected, either positively or negatively, and you may need to keep your own Emotions in check as you lead others that will have their own version of how they are affected. Working through the REAR Steps of an Ending is an opportunity for leaders to look after their own foundational wellbeing. It helps prepare for the kinds of conversations that can feel inauthentic or loaded with guilt when you have the awareness of what's coming that others don't.

Projects are another example of staged Endings. It's sometimes hard to know when a project has actually finished. There might be a launch of something a team has been working on for a significant length of time, but might then be weeks or months more of tying up loose ends and responding to feedback. There is a long tail end of the project that continues for some time before it has fully completed. By this time, the main project energy has fizzled out and some people have perhaps left the project. The timing dissonance creates multiple missed opportunities to mark milestones.

The REAR Four Steps help to acknowledge Endings along the way, and ensure that the end, when it does come, is appropriately acknowledged and marked.

This work might challenge you

We know this can be a vulnerable place to go for us as human beings, let alone as human beings who are managers and leaders of others. This is especially the case if we have not been taught how to acknowledge and navigate this vulnerability.

With this level of complexity and vulnerability, we hope we've illustrated why doing your own work first will help you to be a better leader and enabler of others to process their Endings. And yet for many of us, reflecting on Endings hasn't been in our awareness, let alone something we have allocated reflection time to. So, let's start there, with some exercises designed to raise levels of awareness.

There are no right or wrong answers to these, or indeed any questions in the exercises in the coming chapters – this is all about awareness raising, not judgement making.

Exercise 6: Charting your relationship with Endings at work

This timeline exercise is a way of stepping back to look at a bigger picture of your relationship with Endings as a leader in order to identify potential patterns for you and create future choices.

Begin by taking a landscape piece of paper. Draw a horizontal line across the middle and chart your work Endings and Beginnings from the start of your career until now.

Examples of these could be:
- Change of job – external or internal
- Change of team
- Project completion
- Merger, Acquisition
- New boss
- Change of focus for business

Do add your own to this list if you need to. You could also add your personal ones, for example marriage, having children, moving house.

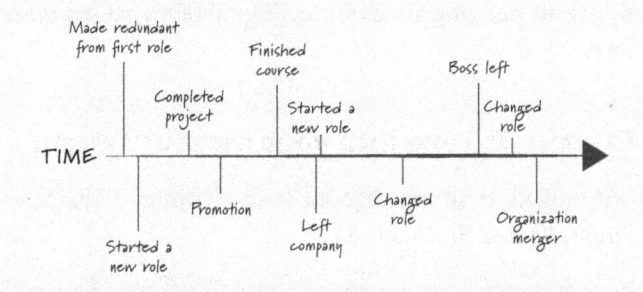

- What do you notice about these Endings, and subsequent Beginnings? There's no right or wrong answer to this – it's simply an opportunity to notice what you notice.
- Typically, how are you with Endings and saying Good Bye?

Let's now look a bit further into your level of comfort and familiarity with Endings.

Look again at:
- What you have chosen to do to acknowledge those Endings?
- Which Endings you are avoiding?

To what extent do you usually take time to reflect on and/or talk through your feelings about events at work?

If this is revealing that you don't spend a great deal of time reflecting on Endings, you are far from alone. It is part of human nature to avoid what brings us pain, or discomfort, to pretend it is not happening, or that our part in it is not important. But if we avoid the pain, we deny the riches of truly acknowledging all of our feelings about what has gone before.

Exercise 7: Tune into your nervous system

We looked at threat responses in Chapter 2 (Fight, Flight, Freeze, Flock, etc.).

In this exercise we are observing and identifying the 'Fs' that may be present. This exercise is about creating curiosity and raising questions. It is also about spotting opportunities to 'check in' and support. Take care, as in all this work, not to turn observations into assumptions. We are looking for insights; it doesn't mean we're right. What it does give us is an opportunity to ask questions, offer support or maybe seek support ourselves. It's an opportunity to think about how we as leaders might have ignited those threat responses, and what we might be able to do to calm them.

- With one Ending in mind, note which Fs may be at play
- Reflect on what you think the impact of those Fs will have been on you, and others
- What have you observed?
- What are the opportunities to settle and support?
- (Flick back to page 29 for a reminder of the triggers for threat responses (the Fs), and some examples of what you might see, hear and experience when those Fs are at play.)

Exercise 8: A deeper dive into the Endings happening now

Building on the work you did in Exercise 4, let's take a closer look at your current relationship with Endings at work. We'll do this by looking again at the Endings in your organization in the recent past and those coming up in the near future.

1. First, refer back to Exercise 4 where you wrote down every Ending that has happened over the past three months in your organization. Think: joining and leaving, team changes, projects, mergers, physical relocations.

2. Remember this isn't a test, it's a raising of awareness. Notice how much time, energy and thought you put into each of them.
   - How much time did you allocate for thinking about and preparing for them?
   - Are there some kinds of Endings that were thoroughly planned?
   - Did some almost go unnoticed?
   - Were there any you tried to avoid?
   - Which ones did you feel very comfortable with?
   - Which ones are you proud of?
   - Were there any you were worried about at the time?
   - Are you still worrying about any of these now?
   - What do you sense in your body as you reflect on these questions? Things like a churning stomach, a tight jaw, tiredness or changes in your breathing, for example.
   - What might those physical sensations be telling you about how you feel?

3. Now, let's apply the same thinking to upcoming Endings. Write down every Ending that is coming up in the next three months.

- How much time have you allocated for thinking about and preparing for them?
- Are there some kinds of Endings that are thoroughly planned, and some that almost go unnoticed?
- Are there any that you are trying to avoid?
- Are there any you feel very comfortable with?
- Are there any you are proud of?
- Are there any you have been worried about?
- What do you sense in your body as you reflect on these questions? Things like a churning stomach, a tight jaw, tiredness or changes in your breathing, for example.
- What might those physical sensations be telling you about how you feel?

In the next chapter you'll find more exercises that give you the opportunity to use the REAR Four Steps to work through your examples of Endings in order to get some further understanding and insight.

Looking back to look forward

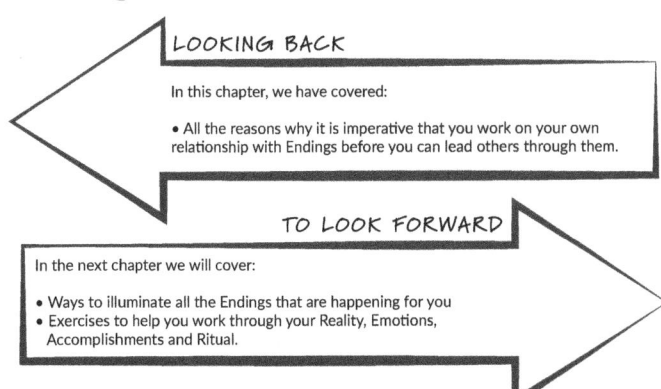

LOOKING BACK

In this chapter, we have covered:

- All the reasons why it is imperative that you work on your own relationship with Endings before you can lead others through them.

TO LOOK FORWARD

In the next chapter we will cover:

- Ways to illuminate all the Endings that are happening for you
- Exercises to help you work through your Reality, Emotions, Accomplishments and Ritual.

Chapter 4

Your first Steps

Sticking with you first, these exercises are designed to help you work through your own Reality, Emotions, Accomplishments and Ritual.

Step 1: REALITY: NAMING IT

One of the great paradoxes of human experience is that we can't change ourselves or our circumstances until we accept what exists right now.

Susan David

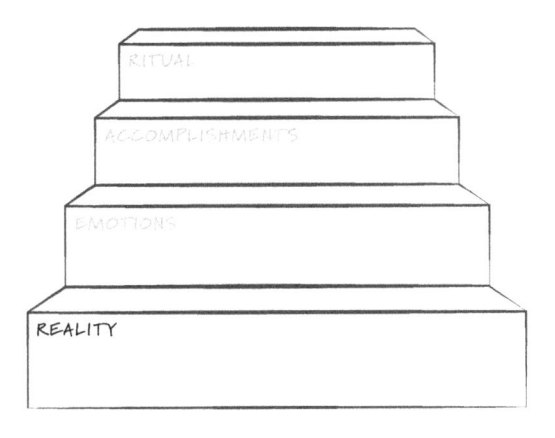

Doing your own work on naming the Reality of a particular Ending will help you to ground yourself as a leader and anticipate and Step into other people's shoes with humility, and clarity of what is needed from you.

It may be that Emotions come up for you as you name the Reality. We encourage you to note those, in the knowledge that Emotions is the second Step, and then come back to the Reality. Trying to keep the Emotion out of the Reality can be helpful because our Emotions can cloud our judgement about what we include.

For example, if a leader was frustrated about the fact that they didn't win a pitch they could easily get stuck in the Emotion of how unreasonable the brief was, and how little work someone else did compared to them and how much longer the winning company had to prepare. Those are all part of the Reality and need to be noted, but there may well be much more to that. As Susan David says, 'In scripting our own stories, we take liberties with the truth'. These might be aspects of the Reality that get missed out because the thoughts are caught up in the bits that felt unfair. The knock-on of that is that when aspects of the Reality aren't acknowledged, opportunities to learn lessons can be missed, including what part you, the leader, might have played in it. The aim is to expand your Reality, get the full picture and all the facts.

Consider: *Have you named it all?*

It's often then worth a longer look at the tricky and messy stuff.

Tricky and messy stuff: illuminating it all

Here are some examples of the tricky and messy stuff that leaders we work with have encountered.

Consider: As you read these examples, what do you notice in relation to the Endings you have been thinking about?

Differences in where the Ending starts from: within one Ending there could be many different starting points. For example, a restructure might mean the starting point for one person is a promotion, and for another that their job is now at risk. A project about to complete might mean some people preparing a pitch for new work, while others are moving to a different team.

Timing dissonance: depending on when Endings are announced and revealed, different people, including you, will have had different information at different times. Therefore, you may have had more time and opportunity than others to process your reactions, think forward and understand your feelings.

Agency: it feels very different when you have been part of the decision-making, versus when you feel unable to influence this Ending or outcome. Who had agency? Who was being told?

Conflicting roles: for example when:

- someone has been promoted, taking with them some of their existing team with whom they have more familiarity, trust and loyalty
- someone is now line managing a close friend

- several people whose budgets need reducing, all of whom believe their contribution matters most.

Job security: for example, in a restructure, some people's future is secure, and they have benefited from the restructure, whilst others are in roles that are at risk. In both cases, leaders are required to manage their own feelings, remain impartial and take account of other reactions and feelings.

Compromise agreements: not all information is available to all people, leaving some with questions; this risks cynicism or people making up their own truths.

Here's an exercise – you might want to look at the example following the exercise before having a go yourself. It's an example that characterizes the types of responses we had when we did this work with a team.

It can be hard to know where to begin with naming the Reality so we find the metaphor of a book useful here.

Exercise 9: Using a metaphor to bring Reality to life

- If the Ending you are thinking about was a book, what would the title be?

- Who are the significant characters? What were their roles in how this Ending came about?
- What are the significant chapters called? (Chapters could relate to particular events, teams or individuals, timing, processes – it's a way of naming the component parts of the Ending.)
- What feels tricky or messy? (Flick back to page 53 if you need a reminder of what we mean by tricky and messy stuff.)
- What's your concluding summary statement of Reality (facts only).

Defeat from the jaws of victory – the book exercise in action

Jacqueline is the Chief Executive Officer (CEO) of a bio-tech startup that was bought by a global tech company on the promise of funding the research and development that would ensure their product successfully went to market. After the agreed two years of investment and continuing research, a competitor put a similar product on the market, six months ahead of Jacqueline's company. The holding company almost immediately ceased investment and started proceedings to divest themselves of the project. Jacqueline worked through the Reality book exercise with her team. They found it cathartic and helped them to move forward and plan for the future. It even raised a much-needed laugh and enabled them to bring humour and perspective into what felt like a devasting situation.

If the Ending you are thinking about was a book, what would the title be?

Between them, they came up with three titles:

1. *Bloody hell, we were so close!*
2. *Those bastards pulled the rug!*
3. *Defeat from the jaws of victory!*

Who are the significant characters? What were their roles in how this Ending came about?

- Jacqueline – CEO of the original bio-tech startup – defending and negotiating with the holding company
- Jacqueline's team – loyal to the ideas and vision – desperately trying to drive faster
- The holding company and the cast of characters within it – alternately and unpredictably engaged, then distant, on repeat
- The rival company – not even on anyone's radar until they made their announcement.

What are the significant chapters called? (Chapters could relate to particular events, teams or individuals, timing, processes – it's a way of naming the component parts of the Ending.)

- Jacqueline's 'Eureka!' moment
- The iterations of the invention
- Jacqueline builds a team
- The long road to funding
- The future is bright
- Wobbles along the way
- Falling off the cliff edge…
- …And no safety net.

What feels tricky or messy? (Flick back to page 53 if you need a reminder of what we mean by tricky and messy stuff.)

- Some of the team are being retained by the holding company, others have been made redundant
- Two members of the team are married, both are being made redundant by this process
- There's an unease that the rival product bears striking similarities to this one that is creating rumour and conjecture about the holding company's confidentiality.

What's your concluding summary statement of Reality? (Facts only.)

The project and product are no longer viable. It had been a source of excitement and pride for a number of years. It was pipped at the post by a rival company and product and there is no time to get it to market as a viable competitor. The holding company is absorbing/dissolving Jacqueline's firm and the team in its current form will no longer exist.

Answering these questions often reveals far more complexity in the Reality than had previously been recognized. We can see from this work on Reality that to lead people through the multiple realities you have identified requires an emotionally literate leader.

You'll notice the lack of Emotions acknowledged here. That is a deliberate part of the process. A number of times in doing this exercise, Jacqueline and the team talked about how they felt. We continued to reassure them that we would do the work of naming and processing the Emotions but, in staying with the Emotion, there is a risk of getting stuck in it. Fully airing all the aspects of the Reality means we can be fully aware of what needs attention. Naming all the aspects of the tricky and messy stuff means that there is a more thorough exploration of what different team members are feeling. This ensures that everyone's feelings are acknowledged, and they have the opportunity to do the work they need to do in order to end well.

Step 2: EMOTIONS

Intellect cannot work at its best without emotional intelligence.

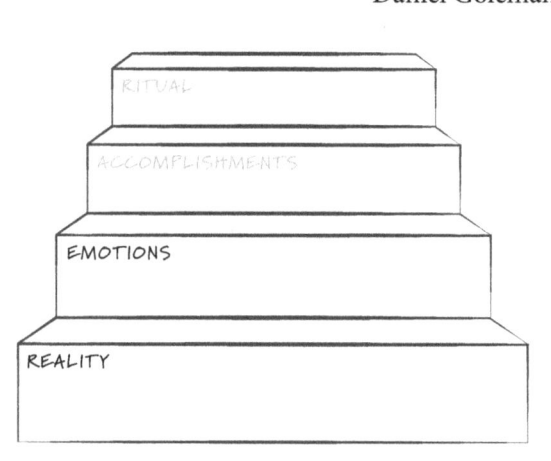

Daniel Goleman

[Diagram of a four-tier stepped pyramid with tiers labelled from bottom to top: REALITY, EMOTIONS, ACCOMPLISHMENTS, RITUAL]

We all have a different access to our Emotions; we feel them differently and have a different range. Some Emotions are familiar and comfortable. Some may feel unfamiliar, as though they are not allowed or not welcome in some way.

Given that looking at Endings invites us to Step into many of our Emotions – loss, grief, celebration, sadness, relief, love and joy – this work might feel uncomfortable and make you feel vulnerable. For example, you may be uncomfortable with expressed anger. Though acting out of anger is rarely a good idea, getting in contact with it to understand the boundaries that might have been crossed is really useful in order to acknowledge and move through it.

Emotions, as we repeatedly say, are at the heart of this work. So much about Endings and a Good Bye is about Emotion. We can tend to group Emotions into positive and negative. The risk – as Brené Brown says – is that 'you can't selectively numb emotions'. Avoiding naming fear-based Emotions (such as disappointment, resentment and regret) will have an impact on how fully we recognize or acknowledge some of the love- and happiness-based Emotions. Kim Cameron notes in *Positively Energizing Leadership* that 'Common human experience, as well as abundant scientific evidence, supports the idea that negativity has a place in human flourishing'.

This work embraces the challenge and benefits of stretching your emotional range and becoming a more emotionally intelligent leader that is comfortable with all Emotions.

Identifying the Emotions involved

Exercise 10: Get in contact with all that you are feeling

With the Ending you are currently working on:
- Write all of these Emotions (and any more that spring to mind as you do so) on separate pieces of paper and place them randomly on the floor

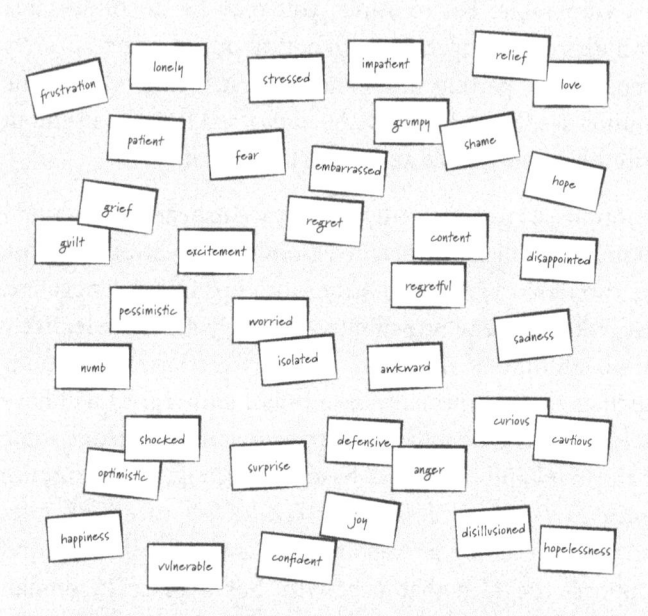

[A scattered arrangement of emotion labels: frustration, lonely, stressed, impatient, relief, love, patient, fear, grumpy, shame, embarrassed, hope, grief, regret, content, disappointed, guilt, excitement, regretful, pessimistic, worried, sadness, numb, isolated, awkward, shocked, defensive, curious, cautious, optimistic, surprise, anger, happiness, joy, disillusioned, hopelessness, vulnerable, confident]

- Walk around the Emotions and, with curiosity and an open mind, notice which Emotions stand out for you? Which have you felt in relation to this Ending?
- What do you sense in your body as you reflect on these questions? Things like a churning stomach, a tight jaw, tiredness or changes in your breathing, for example.
- What might those physical sensations be telling you about how you feel?
- Looking at the ones you have chosen – which of these Emotions did you expect to see? Which surprised you?

NB: On page 175 you'll find a link to our Good Bye facilitation kit that includes a set of Emotions cards.

Name the losses

Unresolved loss is cumulative and cumulatively negative.

John James and Russell Friedman

An additional Step can be to look in more detail at the Endings that stand out for you by naming the losses that were involved.

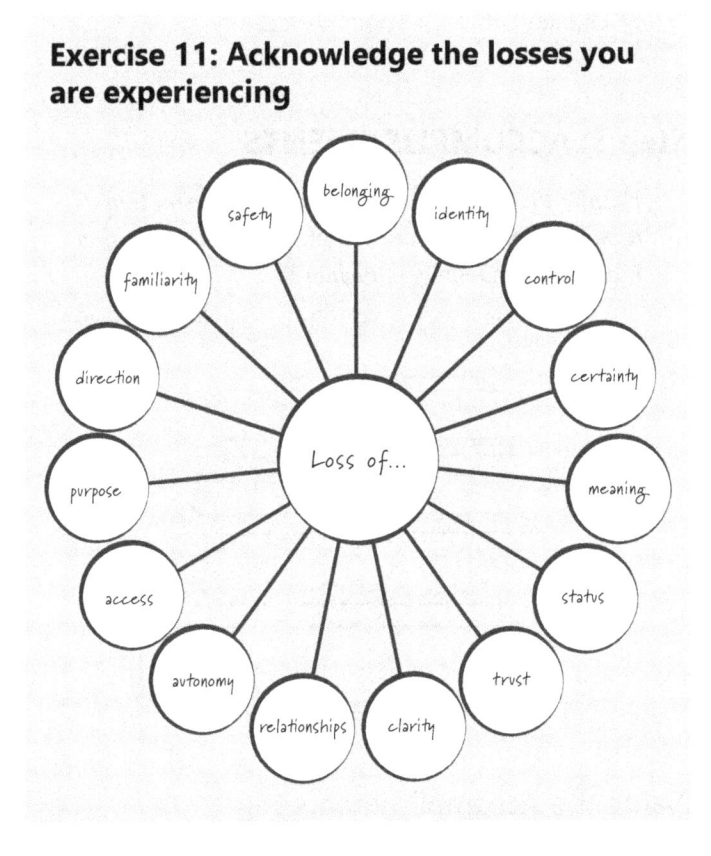

Exercise 11: Acknowledge the losses you are experiencing

Loss of...
- safety
- belonging
- identity
- control
- certainty
- meaning
- status
- trust
- clarity
- relationships
- autonomy
- access
- purpose
- direction
- familiarity

Here are some examples of what we might lose as a result of an Ending:
- With the Ending you are working on in mind, what are the losses you are experiencing?
- How do you feel about them?
- To what extent do the Emotions you identified in Exercise 10 correlate to the losses you have identified here?
- Did any other Emotions surface?

Step 3: ACCOMPLISHMENTS

Despite the power of recognition and affirmation as a basis of building connection, the evidence is that most people do not get much of it.

Jane Dutton

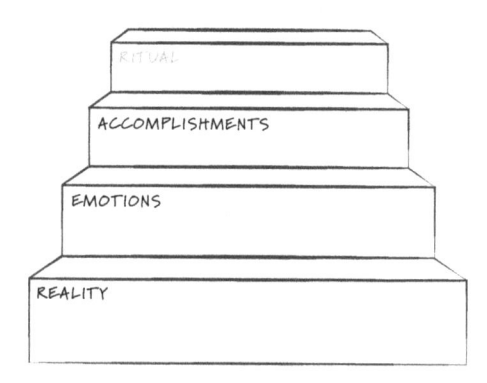

Name the Accomplishments

Continue reflecting by thinking about what you did accomplish. We encourage you to think about both what

you accomplished and how you contributed. Sometimes, our focus is narrowed into the Accomplishments that took place just before the Ending. Take care to widen your perspective and consider all the Accomplishments that came before the Ending became apparent. This way you are disentangling any strong feelings you have about the Ending from the Accomplishments that are yours. These will remain yours and are absolutely true regardless of how you feel about the Ending or how things came to an end.

For some, this can be uncomfortable having been taught not to 'blow our own trumpet'[6] or whatever your local equivalent of that is. Knowing your own Accomplishments does not diminish anyone else's.

A favourite quote of ours is: 'It's not bragging if you can back it up' (Muhammad Ali). This is about you acknowledging your own Accomplishments. It's not for sharing or publishing unless you want to, but by taking this Step of naming your Accomplishment, you are much more likely to be able to access the confidence, pride and energy that stems from knowing them. It also means that you will be far better placed to identify and name other people's Accomplishments when you start working with your team, and to role model to them the OK-ness of knowing and owning your Accomplishments.

Work now through Exercise 12 which will help you to acknowledge your Accomplishments. We encourage you to keep this somewhere you can easily turn to and add more as new things come into your head.

---

[6] In the UK, if you were told not to blow your own trumpet, you were being told not to show off – to keep your accomplishments, and indeed your pride in them, to yourself.

Exercise 12: Own what you have Accomplished
- What did you contribute?
- What are you proud of in terms of what has come to an end?
- What strengths and skills did you use?
- What did you learn and how have you grown?
- What is your legacy, however incomplete?

Here's another way into this, if modesty is getting in your way:

Exercise 13: Channel your cheerleaders

Think of three of your biggest fans who have witnessed you through your involvement in this. What did they say about your contribution and Accomplishments during this time? Or if you don't know what they said, you can imagine it – that counts too.
- What do you think they would say if they were asked to describe your Accomplishments?

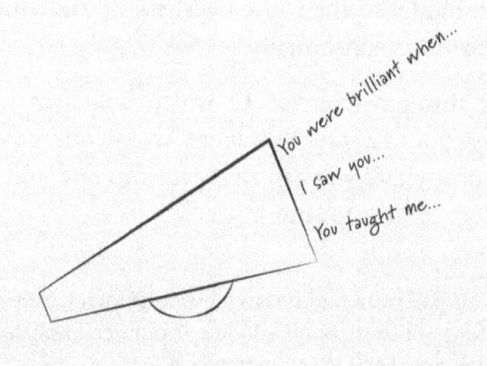

You were brilliant when...
I saw you...
You taught me...

Step 4: RITUAL

If handled well, the experience of an Ending, despite feelings of sadness and grief, can foster personal satisfaction and self-reliance.

Jarlath Benson

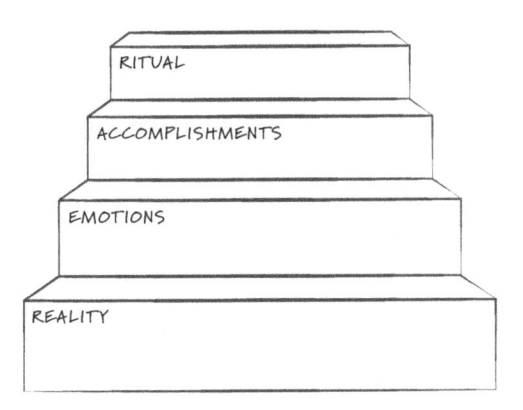

```
RITUAL
ACCOMPLISHMENTS
EMOTIONS
REALITY
```

Having paid attention to the first three Steps we can turn our attention to the myriad of ways we can say a proper Good Bye to something and, in doing so, be able to turn our energy and attention more fully to the future. A Ritual can be anything, big or small, public or private, that meaningfully marks a moment. It doesn't need to be a grand gesture to be significant. It might, for example, be writing something down, saying something out loud, adding an object to your desk, or an image to your screensaver, or a coffee with a friend or colleague. Or bigger examples might include travelling to a specific destination or visiting a meaningful monument. It could be a huge party, or a dinner somewhere special with important people who toast and mark the moment with you.

> ***Consider:*** *What examples of Rituals or marking the moment have you witnessed or been part of at work?*

As long as a Ritual means what it needs to mean to you, and marks the moment in the way you need, it's yours to choose how you do it. There are two parts to this: working out what's possible, and then choosing one that is meaningful.

The next exercise will help you to identify the possible Rituals that will hold meaning for you.

Exercise 14: Exploring Ritual possibilities that resonate for you

- List all the ways you have heard any kind of ending being acknowledged. You could ask other people for their examples as well.
- How do you like to mark an Ending?
- What Rituals would offer acknowledgement of an Ending amid some of the messy and tricky stuff? And what might honour the Accomplishments you noted in Step 3?

The next exercise, based on *The Artist's Way* by Julia Cameron and *The Write Place* by Karyn Prentice and Elaine Patterson, is designed to get you thinking with both breadth and depth about making the Ritual meaningful.

Exercise 15: Creative ways to generate ideas for your Ritual

For this exercise you will need a timer and some paper.

Put this question at the top:

What matters about marking this Ending?

Set a timer for three minutes and, with this question in mind, write or draw without stopping. This doesn't have to make sense or be well crafted. It's about getting your thoughts down on paper in a stream of consciousness.

After the three minutes is up, take a minute to look at what you have written and circle three words or short phrases that feel important to you. Don't overthink it – go with your gut.

Now set another timer and repeat the stream of consciousness, this time using your three circled words as the starting point.

After three minutes do the same again. Circle three words that feel important.

Now write for a final three minutes about those words.

Finally, circle or underline three more words or phrases.

Now look back through the possibilities you generated in the first part of this exercise, and also take a moment to look at the words you have highlighted in this part. Finally, take a final minute to write a line of wisdom or advice to yourself about what you have noticed about marking this moment and how you want to do that.

Having worked through one Ending in depth you will be better aware and equipped to lead others through Endings. The more you repeat the REAR questions and exercises in relation to different Endings, the more awareness you'll generate.

You may have noticed in doing this work that a previous Ending you may have experienced at work is still having an impact on you, even if that Ending was a very long time ago. It's never too late to work through an Ending and the REAR Four Steps can be used for an old as well as a current Ending. A client we worked with noticed how often she felt stuck in thoughts and memories of the way she had been treated in a previous organization and that it was having an impact on her wellbeing, decision-making and energy. Using REAR reflections she was able to, for the first time, say out loud every aspect of what had happened. This included the messy stuff, how she felt and all that she had accomplished before the mess of the Ending. The Ritual she chose was to write herself a letter fully expressing how she felt about the Ending and ceremonially throw it in the bin.

So that's one more Ritual option for you. Write a 'letter that doesn't get sent' – one that acknowledges all Four Steps.

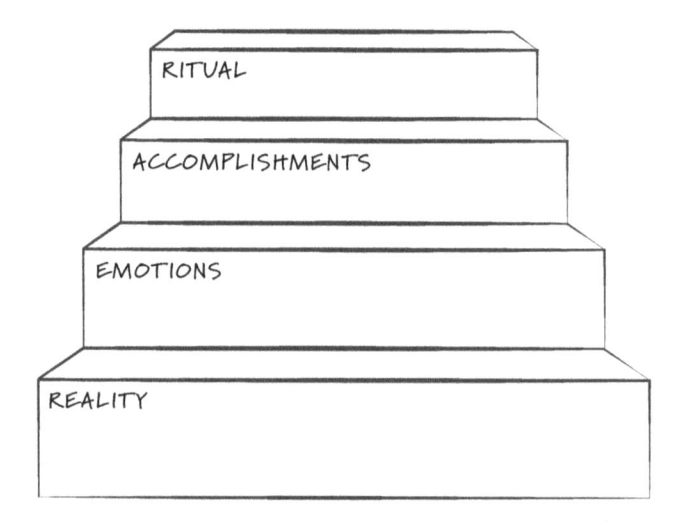

Looking back to look forward

LOOKING BACK

In this chapter, we have covered:

- Ways to illuminate all the Endings that are happening for you
- Exercises to help you work through your Reality, Emotions, Accomplishments and Ritual.

TO LOOK FORWARD

In the next chapter we will cover:

- How to effectively lead your team through Endings using the Four Steps: Reality, Emotions, Accomplishments and Ritual
- Reflecting on how others' experience of the Endings might differ from yours, and what their needs might be.

A half-time listening interlude

If there is one skill that is crucial to working with Endings, and that we want to help you master in support of this work, it's the skill of listening. Really listening, not waiting to speak.

> *Our impulse to be helpful often overrides the need to begin by taking stock.*
> Dr Kathryn Mannix

These pages are an interlude between your work on yourself and your work with others. They are an opportunity to work on your listening skills in service of your work on Endings.

For many of us, the fact that we are hearing leads us to assume that we are really listening, even though sometimes isn't the case. One leader who worked with us was reflecting on the proportion of time spent paying more attention to the voices in their own head than the voices of their colleagues and was shocked by what the small self-auditing exercise revealed about the quality of attention they were paying to their colleagues. In their words, 'This isn't pretty!'.

So many things can contribute to a lack of focus on the person we are listening to. For example:

- Lack of clarity on the purpose of the meeting or conversation

- Lack of clarity on our roles in this conversation
- Other pressing matters at work
- The length of the to do list
- The email notifications flashing up on screen
- Irritation at someone else in the room
- Irritation at the person you spoke with before you came into the room
- Formulating the best way to say the next thing you want to say and waiting for the chance to say it
- Worry about the meeting you have to go to after this one
- Hunger
- Fatigue
- Children texting about forgotten school books
- Conversation in a language that is not your mother tongue.

We can be kind to ourselves on being distracted – we're human and we all do it. The question is how often and is it too often? And, having realized you need to return your attention to the room, how do you do that?

We have acknowledged already the vulnerability and breadth and depth of feelings that can potentially be present in conversations about Endings. To be leaders that are trusted to have these conversations, we need to be listening.

Here are some ways to enhance or maintain our leadership listening skills, starting with some things you can do if you find your attention wandering during an Endings conversation.

Exercise 16 : Listen better!

Listen to a podcast and choose to move from passive listening to active listening by setting a timer and listening for one minute with the intention to repeat back what has just been said. You can also use podcasts to practise listening for subtext and the things that are unspoken. Listen for what you think is being said or thought in the pauses. Listen to formulate questions that further your understanding of what you are hearing.

We also recommend the work of Nancy Kline, Susan Scott and Dr Kathryn Mannix to support your listening skills.

Exercise 17: Preparing yourself to listen

Before a meeting, note down potential distractions on a piece of paper and literally leave them somewhere to pick up again later.

Minimize distractions – turn off notifications, deal with that emotional niggle from how you left the house this morning, eat something, drink some water – take responsibility for the energy you bring to your capacity to listen.

Be clear on the purpose of the meeting and your role in it (look back at the exercises in Chapter 3 for clarity on this) then set a listening intention in relation to your role. To be most useful to others in this meeting, what should I be listening for? And what can I ask others to listen for?

Note where you are in relation to this Ending by comparison with others you are talking to. Be mindful of any differences between the amount of information you hold, and the amount of time you have held it.

Allocate time for the conversation, and choose the space, in a way that supports the quality of the conversation that is needed and helps you to listen.

Exercise 18: Being present – getting back in the room

Breathe out. Controlling the out breath will help you control your state and in turn quieten the distracting voices in your head, supporting you to return your attention to other people.

Listen to repeat back. Choose to focus intently enough on what you are hearing that you'd be able to repeat it back. Listening to repeat or summarize means you are requesting something of yourself that will increase your focus.

Listen for what's not being said. Listen closely enough to hear themes, sub-text, hints, feelings. As Susan Scott says, 'We may succeed in hearing every word yet miss the message altogether'.

Remind yourself of the purpose of the meeting or conversation and your role in it. What should someone in your role, in this meeting, be listening for? Remind yourself of that and listen for it.

Be truthful and curious. Get curious with yourself, and potentially with the others in the room, about what is causing you to be distracted, and indeed whether there is something useful in that. This could be anything from the need for a break, to revealing that you have collectively drifted away from the purpose of the meeting, or maybe didn't have a clear enough one in the first place. It could reveal that there are some issues in how you work together and talk to each other that need to be addressed before you get stuck in to the content. Rather than fight the distraction, ask yourself what it means and how in turn that information is useful.

Usually the brain that contains the problem also contains the solution – often the best one.
Nancy Kline

Now let's look at some ways to work on your listening skills in preparation for conversations about Endings, and to support your leadership listening in general. Here's an exercise based on Nancy Kline's work that you can use with your team to support the quality of attention you pay to each other. As it's a longer and more complex exercise, we've broken it into sections for you to get clear on before embarking on it.

It requires a facilitator that can be you, or someone else in the team. We have offered an example based on Endings, but you can adapt this exercise to work on your listening across any leadership team topic.

Exercise 19: Listening as a team

The purpose of this exercise is to provide a thinking environment for one member of a group or team to help move them forward with an issue. The purpose is not to offer solutions. Moving to solutions too quickly can stifle expanding the individual's thinking.

Once insights have been offered, the individual chooses which questions/enquiries they would like to discuss further or hear more about.

Facilitator's Guide (also available in the Good Bye Facilitation Kit at GoodByeCoach.co.uk).

One person in the group is made the facilitator. It is helpful for the facilitator and the person bringing the issue to be different people if possible, to ensure that the group stays within the process and to generally facilitate the session.

The group's full attention is on the individual and the question they have posed. The facilitator keeps an eye on time and encourages the group to stay on task and honour the process.

Set up:
The facilitator begins by explaining the structure and format using the following prompts:
1. Our focus as a team is on expanding the individual's thinking in relation to this Ending
2. We will spend 20 minutes (or whatever timing you agree) on this exercise
3. To begin, I (as facilitator) will ask a series of questions (these are set out after item 6) that help

the individual to share the issue they would like to explore
4. We will listen first, without interruption, and then take it in turns to offer our insights.
5. After we have heard from the individual we will offer insights (NB. This can either be done by taking turns or by taking a share-when-ready approach; either works, but agree beforehand which approach you will take). I will encourage the whole group to offer an insight. The focus individual remains quiet until all insights have been offered.
6. Insights can come in the form of:
   - Questions
   - Sharing of our own relating or connected experiences
   - Saying what we are curious about or what we have noticed
   - Offering themes, connections or language that stood out.

Facilitator questions and notes:
1. What Ending (or what aspect of this Ending) do you want to think about in this session? Allow the individual to speak until they run out of steam
2. Is there anything more (you think or feel or want to say about this)? Don't be tempted to miss this Step; the individual is processing as they say it out loud. Repeat the question until they say they are done.
3. What do you want the session to achieve at this point? It can be helpful to playback and clarify a

few times until it is a precise question; this focuses the individual and helps the group understand what insights to offer.
4. What would be most helpful from the group to help you achieve this? This is asking the individual how they want to use the group and what they need.
5. Who would like to offer an insight? Having understood what the individual is looking for from the group, this is the point at which you start to hear the insights from the group. Encourage offers to be made without attachment. In other words, try to let go of being right or wrong. Try also not to be attached to whether or not the individual finds it useful at this moment. They may do. They may not. It may be useful at a later date that you never know about. Try to offer with the positive intention of expanding their thinking, without the need for anything back.
6. Continue asking the individual what else they would like to discuss or hear more about until either time is almost up, or they have stated that they feel they have heard enough.
7. Towards the end of the session ask the individual to summarize where their thinking has got to, e.g.
    - Can you summarize where your thinking is now?
    - Is there anything you want to commit to doing next?
    - What else do you need from the group?
    - What are you taking away from the session and what else do you need?
8. Thank the team for participating and close the session.

> *In the presence of the question, the mind thinks again.*
>
> Nancy Kline

Leaders and teams we have worked with get enormous value from listening to each other in this way. It builds trust, clarity, empathy and curiosity, all of which play important roles in leading others through the REAR Four Steps and increasing the quality of attention you place on the impact of Endings in your organization. We encourage you to give it a try, and as ever, if you don't feel confident to facilitate this as a leader yourself, engage with a professional who can support you as you are building these skills and building the safety in the team.

Chapter 5

Leading others

We'll begin this chapter with an unapologetic repeat. In our experience as practitioners, trainers and coaches, and people who have been through a lot of self-development, the work you have just done on yourself first is key to how safely and supportively you can lead others through this kind of work. Everyone you work with will have their version of everything you have been uncovering about yourself and working on in Chapters 3 and 4. All the reasons why it was important to you are why it is important to take care of it for others. By starting with yourself you have put yourself in the position to be a more useful leader of others in relation to Endings, both in terms of how you address Endings and lead Endings, and in terms of your raised awareness of the impact an Ending could be having.

By doing this work, you are not only guiding yourself, but the people who are immediately in front of you, other parts of the system, and the people who will come after you. For example, in our experience, someone who occupies a role after someone has left will feel more settled and be more successful (potentially without ever knowing why) if the seat that they occupy has been vacated well.

By attending transparently and thoroughly to an Ending, you lessen the chances of there being secrets, rumours or assumptions that impact trust, joy, relationships and psychological safety.

Architect, messenger or victim?

It is important to acknowledge that leading others through Endings will be different from managing yourself through one. There are many factors that will affect how you feel about the Ending you are leading. For example, you will have had different responsibilities and inputs into the project that has not come to fruition or failed. You may be the architect of a restructure of your team, you may be the unwilling messenger who is tasked by more senior leaders to deliver news of a company-wide redundancy plan – a plan over which you have no control and don't agree with. Therefore, your Reality, Emotions and Accomplishments may well be different. You may well have completed your Ritual before others even know the Ending is on the horizon. The purpose of the next exercise is to get clear on how your role is different from that of your team.

Exercise 20: Think through the relationship between you, others and the Ending
- What is your role in the Ending you are leading?
- Is there timing dissonance between you and your team? How far ahead in time and processing are you from the team?
- What Emotions are uniquely yours and what might be shared?

- What are your Accomplishments before the Ending and in how you are leading the team through it?
- What Ritual serves you well, so you have closed your relationship to the Ending and can now fully serve others?

Use the following matrix to investigate where you and members of the team are right now in relation to what is coming to an end. The vertical axis represents the level of choice and autonomy each party has over the Ending, and the horizontal axis represents you and others. Plotting the level of autonomy for you and other members in the team can help to illuminate differences in how the Ending might be received. It is important to acknowledge whether you were the architect or whether you were equally imposed upon.

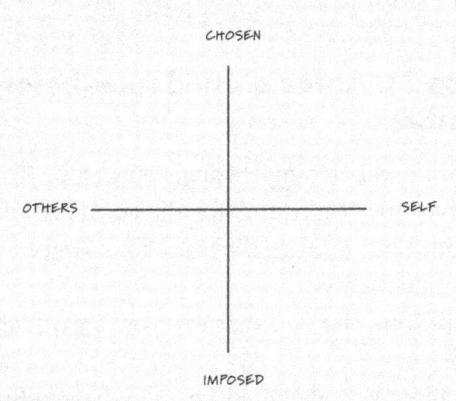

```
                    CHOSEN
                      |
                      |
                      |
   OTHERS ────────────┼──────────── SELF
                      |
                      |
                      |
                   IMPOSED
```

Depending on what you uncover here, you may wish to consider bringing in some external support for working on an Ending with multiple people as this can be sensitive work. It may help if this is facilitated by someone neutral. While our message is about attending to Endings, we are conscious this is not necessarily about you doing this yourselves.

In this chapter we will share more questions and exercises to work through with others. A good place to start is to look back at the exercises on pages 3 and 31 that you used to raise awareness of the Endings that you are navigating, and the relationship between them, as well as your relationship with them. You may want to share some or all of what you have learned about yourself before inviting others to do so.

It's worth noting that when we refer to a team this could be as few as one or two other people.

Ground rules

Exercise 21: Agree ground rules before you embark

We recommend talking through and agreeing some boundaries and behaviours for the conversations you have about Endings with the team, for example:
- Confidentiality
- Respecting the fact that everyone's experience is different
- Listening with the intention of understanding and appreciating someone else's perspective
- No pressure to share.

Once you are ready, here are some ways to zoom in on each Step using the REAR Steps.

Reality

Allow this to be a difficult time and respond with compassion, understanding and acceptance

Jarlath Benson

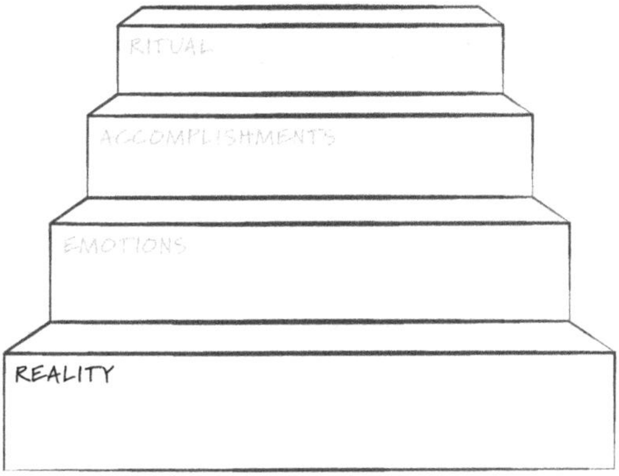
RITUAL
ACCOMPLISHMENTS
EMOTIONS
REALITY

One way of getting greater understanding of the Reality of an Ending's impact on people is to use David Rock's SCARF model (see Chapter 1).

Exercise 22: Two sticky-note ways to use SCARF

You'll need a blank wall!

Place your title at the top – in other words, the Ending that you are looking at. For example, 'Closing Project Green' or 'Restructuring Purple Team'.

Put some words below the title to act as reminders of the Reality.

For example, Project Green formally closes in October. The team has been working on this for nine months. The team is being reallocated to other projects.

Now create a space for each of the five SCARF domains and invite the team to think about (and note) the ways in which each of these domains is being impacted.

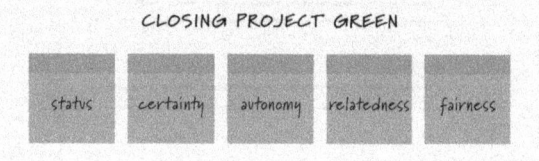

CLOSING PROJECT GREEN

| status | certainty | autonomy | relatedness | fairness |

Alternatively, another row of sticky notes represents names of individuals or groups impacted by the Ending.

Under each name/group, the team adds notes saying which domains they think are impacted for that person.

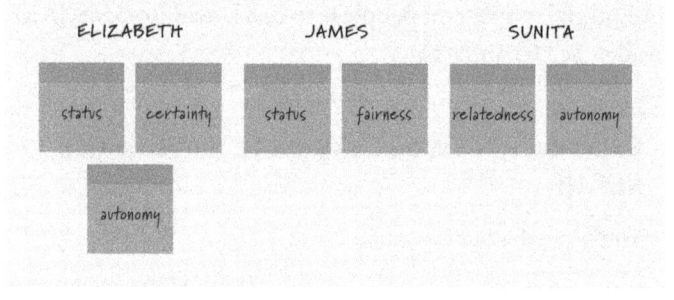

ELIZABETH: status, certainty, autonomy

JAMES: status, fairness

SUNITA: relatedness, autonomy

Taking this time may well change your understanding, increase your empathy and change the way you manage conversations and deal with people. This can help the team get in contact with what is important to them, what elements of the Reality they find particularly unsettling and the ways in which they can start to articulate how they feel.

Remember there is no right and wrong; this is about acknowledging how an Ending will impact each member differently.

It's important to get into the complexities of conflicting, tricky and messy realities. As Susan Scott notes in her book, *Fierce Conversations* (fierce being important, necessary and challenging): 'When Reality changes… and when we ignore competing realities… if we dig our heels in, we fail'.

Uncovering the full Reality – and the range or perspectives on that Reality – makes way for acceptance, empathy, connection, compromise and possibility.

The 'Fs' exercise (Exercise 7) you did in Chapter 3 is also a great one to lead your team through. You can either have each person working quietly through the exercise alongside each other and then compare notes or you can have a large version of it up on the wall and all add sticky notes concurrently, talking it through as you go.

Emotions

A blending of accurate thought and honesty of the heart is not touchy/feely. It is rigorous and professional – and a vital piece of good group thinking.

Nancy Kline

Remember that everyone's emotional compass and sensitivity is different – no Emotions are static. Emotions are impacted by our context, wellbeing and environment – there will be factors within and beyond work in the mix.

Exercise 23 is designed to surface and acknowledge how the team is feeling without getting in to the need to fix or smooth it over.

```
          ┌─────────────┐
          │   RITUAL    │
      ┌───┴─────────────┴───┐
      │   ACCOMPLISHMENTS   │
  ┌───┴─────────────────────┴───┐
  │          EMOTIONS           │
┌─┴─────────────────────────────┴─┐
│            REALITY              │
└─────────────────────────────────┘
```

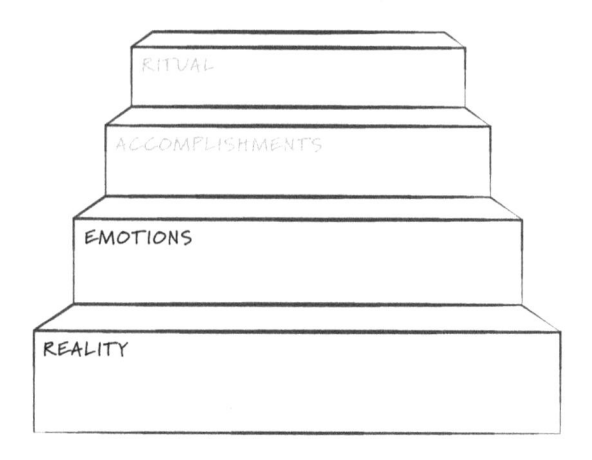

Exercise 23 : Exploring Emotions together

Remember it is useful and important to allow people to express their feelings relating to the Ending in question without making any assumptions or judgement of what is right or wrong.

As this is potentially challenging and sensitive territory, we suggest using a version of the exercise you used for yourself.

Things to consider:

Have an agreement about how to make this OK for everyone. Be prepared to spend time on this before you start – it will be time well spent. For example,

agree with the team that this is about acknowledging solutions rather than trying to fix or find solutions.

Write all these Emotions on separate pieces of paper and place them randomly on the floor. (Or for ease you may want to use our Good Bye facilitation kit that includes a set of Emotions cards.)

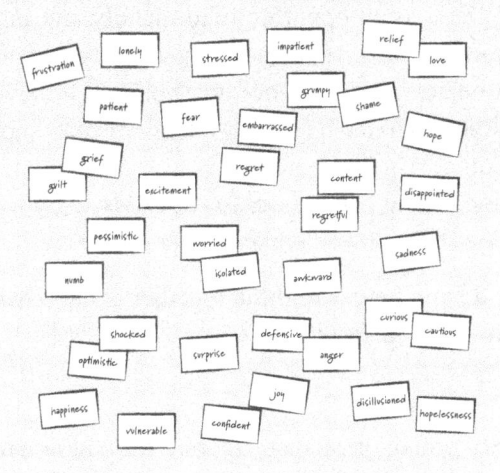

frustration, lonely, stressed, impatient, relief, love, patient, fear, grumpy, embarrassed, shame, hope, grief, regret, content, disappointed, guilt, excitement, regretful, pessimistic, worried, sadness, numb, isolated, awkward, shocked, defensive, curious, cautious, optimistic, surprise, anger, happiness, joy, disillusioned, hopelessness, vulnerable, confident

Collectively, add any others you can think of.

Invite the team to walk around the Emotions, and with curiosity and an open mind, ask them to think about the following questions:
- Which Emotions have you felt in relation to this Ending?
- Which of these Emotions did you expect to see? Which surprised you?

The Emotions that have been identified are then transferred to a sticky-note wall, or you can use a virtual whiteboard to make a word cloud. In this way, you are collectively raising awareness of, and witnessing, the full range of people's Emotions.

You may wish to have a round of requests and offers after this. The rule here is that there is no expectation to

explain, and people can 'pass' if they want to. Although there should be no expectation to explain the 'pass', you could use it as an opportunity to identify any support that you, or one of your team, might need or want; this could be anything from needing nothing, to having a chat over a coffee, to requesting qualified expert support.
- Something I have noticed is…
- Something I would like to request is…
- Something I would like to offer is…

A build from here is to think together about what else people might be feeling.

It's worth noting here that we can feel these Emotions strongly. It's also worth noting the importance of there being no right or wrong. Anger, for example, is a really useful sign that a boundary has been breached or a personal value has been impacted, but many of us can feel it's something we shouldn't express. The irony of that is it comes out in other ways through things like passive aggressive remarks or sarcasm, or it explodes out of us when we're not expecting it. To say 'I feel angry' is a legitimate and important thing to acknowledge that also helps the expression of it be OK for yourself and others. From there, it's possible to look at what other feelings are present. This also highlights how important it is to feel grounded and OK yourself before leading others.

Remember some people find it much easier to access or express Emotions aloud than others do. Everyone has different access, intensity and expression. Therefore, it is important to respect everyone's choice of what and how to share, if at all.

One way to do this exercise that supports those who find it hard to share, and helps us to refrain from rescuing and fixing, is to do this exercise in silence. To do this, simply stop once the Emotions have been placed on the wall and allow some time for people to reflect quietly. In our experience this can be even more powerful than discussing it.

Accomplishments

> *Organizations and leaders [reveal] the value they give to relationships by their choices of people to thank and how they thank them.*
>
> Jane Dutton

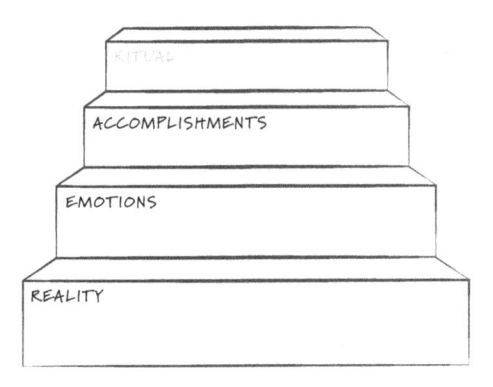

Once the team members have acknowledged the Reality and had an opportunity to explore and express how they feel, it is important to capture what has been achieved.

Take the time to express and acknowledge what you are proud of in relation to what came before this Ending.

Remembering that Endings can be messy, drawn out, not of our making or not fully welcome, it is therefore important to go back to a time before the Ending became a possibility to look at Accomplishments. This is vital for the individual and team's sense of self, pride, dignity and capability. It therefore impacts their wellbeing and resilience going forward.

There is a significant and growing body of evidence from the field of Positive Psychology that appreciation and acknowledgement of contribution has an impact on both individual and organizational health and wellbeing. As we have noted previously, it is so easy to assume that people are feeling seen, heard and valued. This exercise supports making sure that no stone of appreciation is left unturned.

Exercise 24: It only takes a minute

1. In a team meeting, take five minutes to all note down and share what has been achieved in a project or pitch, and whether it has been successful or not.
2. Take time to thank a colleague who is leaving the team with specific feedback and appreciation of what they have meant to you.
3. As a team, take it in turn to share what you are most proud of in relation to the Ending. The other team members listen for qualities, skills, values and strengths of each speaker, and offer them as feedback. You can record these as you go on a postcard and hand them in at the end. This gives an enduring reference they can go back to.

Ritual

Completion allows you to return to a full range of human emotions; it means that you don't have to go over the same things again and again.
                                    John James and Russell Friedman

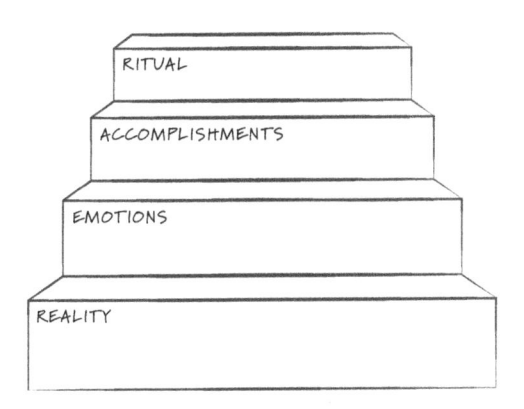

```
┌─────────────────────────────┐
│  RITUAL                     │
├─────────────────────────────────────┐
│  ACCOMPLISHMENTS                    │
├─────────────────────────────────────────────┐
│  EMOTIONS                                   │
├─────────────────────────────────────────────────────┐
│  REALITY                                            │
└─────────────────────────────────────────────────────┘
```

This is the opportunity to collectively say Good Bye to the person, project or possibility. With thought, something magical can be created here, the feeling and impact of which will travel forward with each individual present. The Ritual is the opportunity to say Good Bye, and thank you. It is the antithesis of an OK Bye, or an Ignored Bye. Ritual allows us to truly acknowledge, beyond words, what has come to an end. Marked in many different ways, Ritual finally closes the chapter, ready for the next.

This exercise opens up discussion about how to create a Ritual that is fitting, and meaningful, for the Ending and new Beginning that is emerging. Metaphor is often a great way to encourage and support people to talk.

Exercise 25: Opening the door to the new Beginning

Each member of the team chooses a door that, for them, represents this Ending. After taking some individual time to prepare, they share their responses to these questions:

1. Why did you choose this door? What does it say about what is Ending?
2. What does it say about what is beyond the door?
3. What are the experiences, skills, learning and Accomplishments that you are taking with you as you go through the door?
4. How do you feel as you approach the door? How do you feel on the other side?

This Ritual is an example of what we mean when we talk about Endings for Beginnings. The Ending opens the door to the things that Begin on the other side of it. It can be a very energizing transition and acknowledges that the team's input is complete. It also offers each team member a glimpse of the new bright futures they are anticipating.

Exercise 26: Create the heartfelt leaving speech you would like to receive

The most time-honoured Ritual for an Ending at work is leaving drinks and speeches. It is an opportunity to put much more thought and care into a significant moment. Think about what is fitting to say about an individual so they feel deeply appreciated whatever the circumstance of the Ending. Consider what stories would be meaningful for them to hear.
- Who is best to contribute?
- What would be meaningful?

This is an area which is often done badly and does more harm than good. Do not rush the preparation or choosing of a gift. A bad speech or gift will live long in the memory; a thoughtful one will send ripples through the whole team.

I don't drink coffee!

Paul, who was leaving the organization he had worked in for the previous ten years, told us the story of the leaving gift his line manager had bought for him with the proceeds of the staff collection. The gift was something he would never choose, let alone use. It was a coffee maker, and Paul didn't drink coffee. This felt crass and insensitive, and he can still remember the feeling of embarrassment as he thanked his boss; he was too polite to say anything else. What he wanted to say was, this shows you clearly don't know me, and you have not taken the time to talk to someone who does know me and who could have aided you in buying a more heartfelt and useful gift.

Hadrian's Wall

A leader who was retiring and loved hiking was given a beautiful acknowledgement by his department who planned a walk along Hadrian's Wall with him. He started the walk with his boss, and his colleagues surprised him by popping up and joining him for various parts of the day's journey along the way. They joined the walk in the order of knowing him, with his most recent colleagues joining him last. As they walked, they shared memories and anecdotes of their time together. The relaxed and leisurely Ritual allowed time and space for true acknowledgement of his Accomplishments, deep relationships and impact he had made on them all. It was planned and spontaneous, light-hearted and moving.

Moving out

An organization was moving out of its founding premises to a new building, more appropriate in size and location for what the organization had become. The leaders wanted to honour all that had taken place within the physical walls of the old premises, despite the shortcomings of the space and facilities. The leadership team gathered in the foyer of the old building and shared their stories of what the building had meant and made possible. They then walked together, in silent contemplation, from the old premises to the new premises. They arrived at the new premises feeling that they had brought the founding spirit of the organization with them, and were ready to embrace all that their new location would make possible.

If you've ever moved house, you'll remember the feeling of leaving a place that has been the home that you have entertained in, grown in, perhaps brought your children home to, perhaps grieved in. This sense of place, space and time in work settings is often far more significant than we give it credit for. Leaving places and spaces can also be a way of creating a simple but powerful Ritual to mark an Ending.

We have witnessed different versions of this during the course of our work, three of which we have outlined next. These are Rituals that people have created to say a brief but heartfelt and personal Good Bye to a room or a building at a significant moment.

Using where it happened to honour what happened

As part of a leadership course, one particular group had done deep work that included reference to their relationships with family and friends and how this informed who they were as leaders. This had led to personal insights and shifts and had been very moving for everyone there. Before they left the building on the last day, they each went into the room and took a moment to acknowledge what they had experienced, how they felt and what they had accomplished. They held a moment of silence and switched the lights off. After pausing for as long as they wanted to, they switched the lights back on, signifying the room being ready for the next person or group. Once they had all done that, the course leader switched off the lights a final time and closed the door. The work then felt complete to everybody.

***

When they left their tiny college rooms that had been their entire living spaces, and indeed their whole world during the Covid-19 pandemic, a group of students emptied the rooms, then all went and sat in the doorways of the rooms, facing onto the landing and told stories and shared memories. They acknowledged the Reality of that time, how it had felt and what they had accomplished in those extraordinary circumstances. By then gathering in the landing to hug and hold hands (something they hadn't been able to do), leaving the rooms open for the next wave of students, they were able to make more peace with the challenging college experience they had had.

***

An elderly relative was leaving their house to move into a flat. It had been a house of many memories and a move that signified a change in their life. Concerned that the Reality wasn't being acknowledged, and that they might regret later not saying farewell to their home, we gently encouraged them to say a few words about living there. And then asked, 'How do you want to leave?' They said, 'I'll lock the door, and turning the key is the way of saying I've left, just like we turn a key to go in'. And with that simple gesture, there was an acknowledgement that made the rest of the day a little less heavily charged, and it all felt about the optimism of the new start, rather than the upheaval of leaving.

The wedding speech

We worked with a leader who was planning a talk to the organization about the discontinuing of a particular product, one that she knew would be surprising for many, and shocking to some, as it was a product that had been so closely identified with their brand. She used the ingredients of the speech she had given at her daughter's wedding to help identify the ingredients of an acknowledgement that would be engaging, moving, respectful and optimistic:

- What they were like as a child, or in this case, why the product was first developed and what the different evolutions of the product looked like over time
- Stories of the impact the product had had
- What people loved about it
- Stories of when things had not gone to plan
- Appreciation of what it had made possible and that things would be different from now
- Hopes for the future.

Looking back to look forward

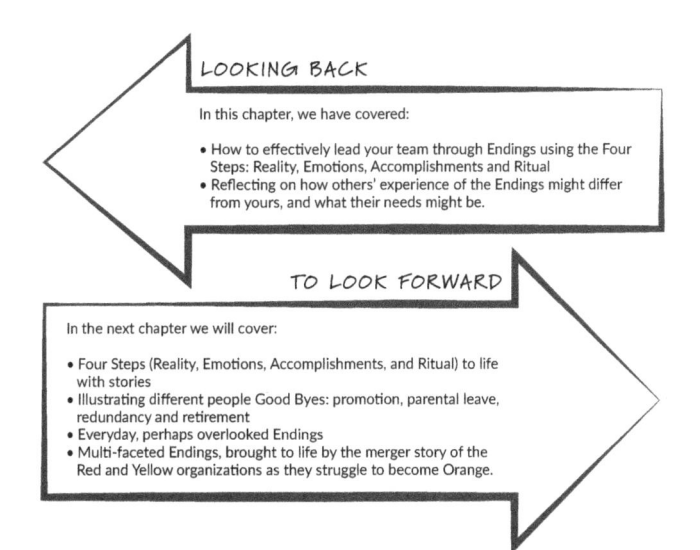

LOOKING BACK

In this chapter, we have covered:

- How to effectively lead your team through Endings using the Four Steps: Reality, Emotions, Accomplishments and Ritual
- Reflecting on how others' experience of the Endings might differ from yours, and what their needs might be.

TO LOOK FORWARD

In the next chapter we will cover:

- Four Steps (Reality, Emotions, Accomplishments, and Ritual) to life with stories
- Illustrating different people Good Byes: promotion, parental leave, redundancy and retirement
- Everyday, perhaps overlooked Endings
- Multi-faceted Endings, brought to life by the merger story of the Red and Yellow organizations as they struggle to become Orange.

Good Bye

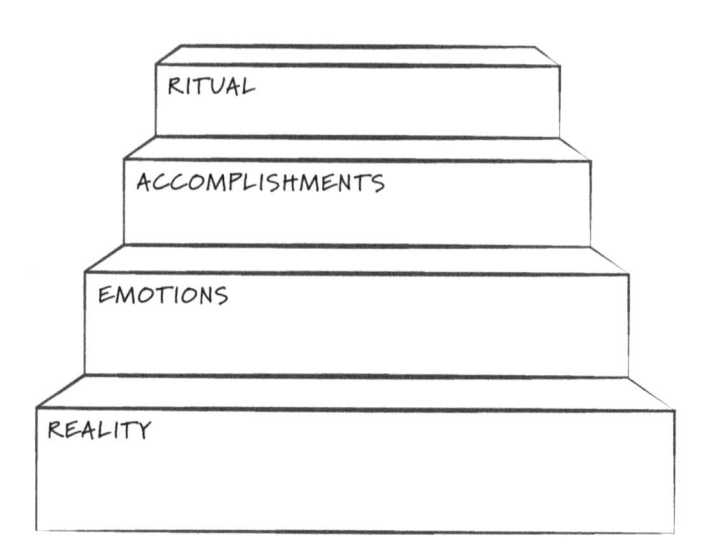

- RITUAL
- ACCOMPLISHMENTS
- EMOTIONS
- REALITY

Chapter 6

Step by step through the Steps

The purpose of this chapter is to help you see how the ideas and exercises we've been sharing so far look and sound in real life. Let's look at what often happens in some examples of different kinds of Endings, and how much better the outcome is when the REAR Four Steps are applied. We'll start with people Good Byes, where the focus of the Ending is an individual. We often find it's the first two Steps, Reality and Emotion, that need more attention in these individual Endings.

Next, we'll look at an example of an Ending that happens regularly for a team, one of the kinds that happen so often and amid so much else in the day-to-day life of the organization that they are glossed over. Project Good Byes are a great example of this. Often, it's a little more focus on the third and fourth Steps, Accomplishment and Ritual, that can make a big difference here.

Lastly, we'll look at a multi-faceted large-scale example in the form of a merger, sharing examples of the impact when leaders are attending to each of the Four Steps, as well as the impact of ignoring them.

People Good Byes

There are People Good Byes happening every day in organizations. Many of those involve an individual leaving the organization. We will look at retirement as an example of leaving later on in this chapter. We're starting with the kinds of Good Byes in which opportunities to end well are sometimes missed because the Ending is a positive one. When a Good Bye doesn't involve leaving the organization, the opportunity to end well is sometimes missed in the excitement about, and the focus on, what's coming next. Promotions and parental leave are both good examples of this. They are Good Byes that, understandably, tend to focus on the Accomplishments and the Ritual, but might miss an opportunity to prepare more thoroughly for the coming weeks and months by taking more time with the Reality and Emotions.

Promotions

When we are coaching leaders who are newly promoted it is common for them to talk about how they are finding themselves sucked back into tasks that their team members should be doing. They are frustrated with their teams that they are not doing these tasks themselves and frustrated with themselves for doing them. The part we uncover with them is that going hand in hand with the frustration, there is also a sense of satisfaction. The completion of these tasks reminds them of the feeling of adding value and feeling competent. Ram Charan et al. drew our attention to this many years ago in their book, *The Leadership Pipeline*, illustrating that this reluctance to delegate, and feelings of failing in the role, are connected to the fact that the leader hasn't fully updated and understood their new measures of success, or celebrated them. Satisfaction therefore comes from doing the things they used to do, that the people they lead should be doing. And it then gets confused and messy, and neither the leader, or those they lead, are feeling fulfilled and successful.

At this point we can work through REAR to help the leader update their measures of success, and fully ground themselves in the Reality of what they are doing, versus what is required of them, and in making changes to their expectations of themselves and their teams. Even better would be not needing to do the updating once things have got difficult, because you have paid attention to REAR early in the role, and ideally before taking up the role.

Some ways to go about this:

1. A promotion involves determining our suitability for a role, applying for the role, updating our CV and familiarizing ourselves with the requirements of the role. We will no doubt talk about what we intend to achieve in the role, and the job description will lay out those expectations. We recommend you take time with the Reality of what you no longer need to do, as well as what you will now need to do.
2. When applying for a promotion and interviewing for a new role you will have naturally thought through and documented your Accomplishments. It is useful to plan how you stay connected to those Accomplishments

as you move into the new role, so that when you are finding your new role challenging, you can feel resourced and energized by your past and get back in contact with your confidence. Reminding yourself of how you achieved them, and the skills and strengths you brought to those Accomplishments, can help you confidently face the new challenge. We encourage our clients to dig into their Accomplishments, and to anchor them in stories, examples, data and the things people have said about them. Regularly doing this supports our resilience when it comes to both Endings and new Beginnings and helps Accomplishments to be something we can access and talk about with ease and confidence.[7]

3. Include the 'future Reality' in your Reality work. How will you define success in your new role? How will you measure success? This is not about the headlines in the job description. It's the more granular day-to-day and week-to-week Reality of what you will need to be thinking, saying and doing that is different from now on. This might include what you will have to delegate no matter how interesting and tempting a project or task is for you to do yourself; how you know in the new role that it has been a good day, or a good week; or how the Reality of your work relationships will change. Leaders sometimes feel as if they are failing or feel unhappy, because they didn't prepare themselves for the Reality

---

[7] In order to use a method of journalling to store and anchor Strengths we recommend the Strengths Stacker Journal that you can find at: www.towardsleadership.com/journals/p/the-strengths-stacker-journal.

of what their working relationships will look and sound like in their new role.

4. Once we start doing this work we might uncover the fact that whilst we are feeling joy, pride and many other Emotions we might normally label as positive when we achieve a promotion, there are other feelings there too, both in the application process and in the early stages of the new role. Acknowledging all the Emotions and spending a little bit of time accepting that all feelings are valid whether they are good or bad, can help us to feel more settled. Ignoring feelings doesn't make them go away. Giving them a name, and maybe some substance, helps to validate them.

Once you have noted all your Emotions, try using this simple sentence to deepen your insight into each one:

I am feeling this because…

The goal here isn't to 'fix' feelings, it's to air them and name them. Doing this will help settle yourself and will give you more insight into how you can best prepare.

Redundancy

In Chapter 1 we looked at why we avoid Endings through both the individual and the organizational lens. As you look through that list of reasons to avoid an Ending, it's easy to see how Redundancy can touch on all of them:

- Pace
- Process
- Entanglements
- Feeling betrayed

- Wanting to fix and rescue
- Facing into loss
- Overly focused on the positives
- Identity
- Leader's capacity to hold Emotion and vulnerability.

We have observed, and directly experienced, how the legal requirement to make a position rather than a person redundant doesn't necessarily feel that way for the person being made redundant. We totally understand there is a process. We understand it's necessary. We do also believe it could often be handled better.

Redundancy is an Ending that is full of tricky and messy stuff, both on an individual and organizational level. This can sometimes result in some glossing over of the truth of how people are feeling, both by the individuals themselves and their organizations.

Sometimes people mean it when they say, 'Redundancies need to be made and I am really happy to take it and I fully appreciate that it's a role that's no longer needed'.

More often the truth that they feel internally is more like one of the following:

- Redundancies are coming – I'm scared I'll be one of them
- Redundancies are coming – I don't mind being one of them but I'd rather not
- Redundancies are coming – I don't believe the position is really going, I think they are trying to get rid of me, and I'll fight this
- Redundancies are coming – I'm leaving anyway but I'll hang on and see if I get paid off

- Redundancies are coming and I have to make them – I feel sick with guilt and I'm losing sleep over having these conversations.

You might have more reactions to redundancy that you'd add to this list. Redundancy is an Ending full of opportunities to have difficult, honest and brave conversations in service of a better experience for all involved.

Whilst much of what we have shared in our other examples of individual Good Byes pertains to Redundancy, there is another nuance around Accomplishments that merits a mention here.

A class act

> *Lucy had an experience that we have heard many similar versions of. During her leaving event, the focus of the speech about her was how well she had handled the redundancy process. Whilst it was good to hear that she had been a 'class act', she was left with the feeling that all that mattered to the leader was how she had managed recent months, and frankly, made their life as a leader easier through her adult and positive response to redundancy. The leader didn't talk about the work that she had done, and her achievements, prior to that point.*

If you, as a leader, are in the privileged and important position of holding someone's Good Bye as a speech maker, take care not to make their Accomplishments all about how they have handled the Ending. It is so important to account for the full contribution that person has made. Account for their entire history in the organization and you will create a healthier Good Bye for them, for you and for anyone listening.

Parental leave

Becoming a parent is a great example of a time when we might feel guilty about acknowledging an Ending. We quite rightly expect this to be a joyous Beginning, but even when it is, there are Endings that come with the territory of becoming parents. A lot of maternity coaching and parental leave coaching tends to focus on the return. We aren't saying that isn't useful and important; it certainly is. Our build is that if we are better prepared for the full Reality of what will change, and of what we are saying Good Bye to, as well as the full range of what we will be feeling, we give ourselves some valuable insight into how it might feel and how it might be. We are then more likely to greet our return-to-work challenges as ones we were expecting to encounter, rather than strangers knocking at the door that we don't want to see!

This is not about preventing change or dampening feelings of joy and celebration. If anything, by acknowledging all our feelings, instead of avoiding those we may have been taught not to talk about, we can feel our joy more freely too, because we haven't put labels and limits on the feelings we 'should' be feeling.

By doing this work, people are able to focus on how they are going to stay appropriately in contact with their organization and not put unnecessary energy into worrying about what they might be missing.

Retirement

Sometimes people coming up for retirement assume they will adjust easily to not working and that because they are looking forward to a change, they will wake up on Day One of retirement feeling great and filling their days. Even so, their last day may feel flat rather than fulfilling, and they may feel disconnected from what they are saying and hearing and are left instead with a lingering and painful sense of themselves, and their work, not mattering.

Our conversations with people who have retired have revealed where the REAR Steps were missed, or glossed over, and could have made for a very different experience:

Reality – They had not fully considered the impact that a different kind of day or week will have not only on themselves, but on their closest relationships.

Emotion – They didn't want to show too much Emotion at work, and didn't want to upset anyone so they keep their feelings to themselves.

Accomplishment – They were proud of what they had achieved but didn't feel as if they should say too much about it for fear of seeming arrogant. They hoped their achievements would be recognized and were looking forward to the speeches, but those speeches didn't actually reflect on the things they felt they had achieved. The words felt like they could have been for anyone.

Ritual – Meanwhile, the organization kept moving at pace and busy people didn't find time to prepare for the farewell. They assumed that the usual drinks and a speech would suffice.

The impact can ripple out beyond the retiring people who left feeling unappreciated, disappointed and sad, and without the energy they expected to have. After an initial week or two of activities, they feel increasingly uncertain about how to use their time and what the future looks like. The lack of acknowledgement can also affect the families of the retirees who can feel resentful of the years they have dedicated to the company for which they worked.

Retirement done well – Rahat's REAR Story

Reality

Rahat has been working as a civil servant for 40 years, his children are grown up and have left home and his wife, who was a physiotherapist, retired two years earlier. She has been keen for him to retire as they have many plans of how they want to go into the next chapter of their lives, including extensive travel and creative courses.

He has been considering all aspects of his life and how they will change, as well as the impact that will have on those around him.

Through exploring and reflecting with a coach he has been able to acknowledge how much of his identity is connected to how he answers the question 'What do you do?' and to be prepared for answering that question differently and comfortably.

A series of exit interviews that the organization has made a standard practice for retiring colleagues has enabled Rahat to dedicate time and space to thinking through the Reality and the implications of this.

The organization also works with retiring colleagues to create a staggered transition. Having stepped down from the department he ran 18 months ago he has been working four days a week on a project close to his heart, which means he feels his legacy is very much as complete as it could be.

By showing this level of awareness and consideration of the full Reality inherent in the retirement experience, as well as how uniquely each individual experiences this process, Rahat has been able to co-create an exit that honours a key moment in life. The organization not only learns from colleagues as they leave and is able to plan how to retain and cascade their knowledge and experience, but they have also noticed how often colleagues refer to this practice in engagement surveys. 'Knowing that the organization cares about the way that I leave, and making that a good experience, increases trust that I am cared for and supported as an individual'.

Emotions

Rahat is aware that he is in a huge transition and whilst he is excited about his plans with his partner, he knows they're going to take some adjusting to. His coach has worked with him on naming Emotions to explore the intensity of those Emotions at different times and in different contexts. This has led to open, honest conversations both at work and at home, including exploring with his partner how they feel about the Reality of this change in both their lives. Seeing the psychologically safe and emotionally intelligent way the organization has supported Rahat has been a source of strength and comfort to his partner, a great example of the way this work ripples out in its reach and impact.

Rahat feels very proud of what he has achieved throughout his career and particularly the last 18 months with his legacy project. He feels grateful to his line manager for co-designing a way to withdraw from running the department to complete the project and end in the way that really honours his skill and contribution. He is hopeful that some of his special relationships and friendships will remain beyond working together. He is wistful about no longer working in the heart of London but is also relieved that he will no longer face the daily commute.

Accomplishments

Because Rahat's Ending is planned and (for him) on time, and he has total agency over it and has had the opportunity to reflect on his career and contributions. Whilst he clears some of his office, he takes time to ponder over colleagues he has worked with, and projects, roles and responsibilities that have spanned his career.

Exit interviews are an opportunity to acknowledge those things, ensuring useful learning is captured and supporting planning for the best possible leaving Ritual. The legacy project ensures a smooth and meaningful mentoring programme is in place for the new graduate entries and means that what he has dedicated his time to over the last 18 months is particularly current in his mind. He reflects on the completeness of going full circle and leaving a legacy to those at the Beginning of their career as he ends his.

Step by step through the Steps

Ritual

Rahat takes time to write to previous line managers, mentors and significant colleagues to thank them for their support over the years. The organization has allocated time for these activities during the last four months of service so that they don't get lost in the high volume of information as handover gets close.

He sees the clearing of his office as an experience to reflect upon this time in the department. His old team purchases a bench for his allotment, and he receives many personal notes of thanks from team members past and present. His line manager makes a very thoughtful speech on his last day for which he had gathered input from many different sources about what they really appreciated and valued in Rahat's leadership. The company gives him and his partner a gift of an easel for their joint new art project of watercolour painting.

In Rahat's example, the impact of paying attention to all Four Steps in a way that is tailored to the individual has helped everybody adjust and end well.

Rahat feels seen and heard, and that his contribution has been valued. Rahat still thinks about his time in the organization, but they are not thoughts he feels bound to in unhelpful ways. He has fully turned towards the interesting things he wants to do next with his life and is engaged with them. It's a beautiful illustration of Susan David's assertion that 'Acceptance is the prerequisite for change. This means giving permission for the world to be as it is because it's only when we stop trying to control the universe that we make peace with it'.

The way that Rahat's retirement has been handled has reassured others that their contribution is valued too, something that is reflected in company engagement scores. Rahat and his former colleagues speak highly of the organization in public and on social media, enhancing the attractiveness of the company to high quality candidates and contributing to high retention rates.

Everyday Endings

There isn't always an opportunity to take a lot of time with an Ending, and the risk is that the lack of time becomes a reason not to pay attention to it at all. Especially when it's the kind of Ending that happens often, like completing a pitch, signing off on or saying no to a project. Whether a proposed team or individual project goes ahead or not, it still marks the end of the preparation, and the beginning of bringing it to fruition, or moving to something else.

The fact that these are everyday Endings means that often time is short. Catch Endings when you can and find quick ways to do something in relation to each of the REAR Steps of Good Bye, or choose which of the Steps would be most useful to pay some attention to.

Pitching for new work is an example of an everyday Ending, some of which are successful and start something, some of which are unsuccessful and never seen again.

No time to pause

> Anna heads up the bid management team for a creative agency. Her role is to coordinate with other functions in the business the bid process for winning new client contracts. They often work under a huge

> *amount of pressure and tight time frames on multiple pitches. When a pitch is won there is great kudos and celebration, thanks are passed down to Anna and her team, with an immediate delivery project plan put in place.*
>
> *When a pitch is not successful the team hardly has time to draw breath as everyone is immediately allocated onto other live projects.*

In Anna's case, because time is short, and this happens so often, it's the Ritual that holds the key to the inclusion of all Four Steps of REAR on a regular basis. Here's an exercise that Anna's team has adopted.

Exercise 27: The Standing Ending

The Ritual is anchored by the fact that at the end of the 'win or lose' point of any bid, there is a Ritual of the team pausing for five minutes to stand together and share feelings about the win or loss. This occurs at the same place in the office. The Reality is shared in the form of time spent and outcome, and there is then an opportunity to share one or two learnings.

Each member of the team then briefly shares how they are feeling and something they appreciate about having worked in this team. Finally, each member of the team states an Accomplishment they are proud of.

This ensures that both wins and losses are given status, and contributions to either are appreciated. It also ensures that one or two learnings are captured every time.

This Ritual is anchored by the fact that it always takes place in the same spot and is time limited.

Multi-faceted Good Byes

One of the most multi-faceted and complex experiences of an Ending that we encounter in our work with organizations is that of a merger and/or acquisition (M&A) of two (or sometimes multiple) companies.

Just some of the Endings that could be at play during this time are:

- Restructured teams, including the leadership team
- Redundancies
- Combining teams
- Closing product lines or projects
- Office or site closures
- Changing branding, including brand names.

We're not suggesting that there is a perfect formula for a perfect Ending in every situation, particularly where an Ending contains multiple Endings and has all kinds of complexity. We are saying that when more attention is paid to Ending using the REAR Four Steps, things are better. And that better, is better.

> *The map is not the territory.*
> Alfred Korzybski

To illustrate this, let's look at a case study exploring examples of missed opportunities, and positive actions that took place during a merger through the lens of a particular team.

We are sharing two very different experiences of a merger from the point of view of the two Finance teams within the two different organizations. Let's call them Red and Yellow.

🌀 Red and yellow don't always make orange

Pre merger, Red and Yellow are teams within separate organizations.

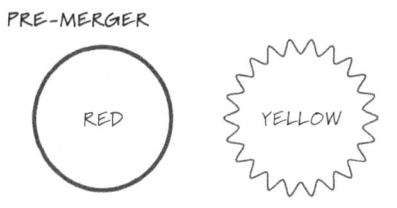

PRE-MERGER

Leaders assumed that post the merger both teams would be seamlessly integrated.

ASSUMED POST-MERGER

Whilst the word merger implies the coming together of two equals, it didn't feel like that.

The Chief Financial Officer (CFO) of the newly merged team was the old red CFO, and the old yellow CFO had been made redundant.

Each of the team members had to go through a process to apply for their new role in the new emerged organization with 50% of them getting a full-time role, 30% of them being made redundant and 20% being kept on as short-term contractors to facilitate the full handover of legacy systems.

The team was still being co-located although the leadership team were based at Red's headquarters, and 'everyone knew' that in the next 12 months Yellow's headquarters would be closed down.

The Red CFO and his leadership team had known what was in store for them, the plans for location and they had agency and design over the process. They had lost loyal members which they were sad about, and had gained new team members from legacy Yellow, some of whom they were concerned wouldn't be up to the job.

The Yellow team had not made or taken the opportunity to get together, and the CFO had left very suddenly with a suspected compromise agreement; they were all rather tentative as to whether she was OK, and no one had made contact.

Two weeks into the new structure, everyone now knew what it meant for them. The past three months had felt very different for the individual team members. There are many different Emotions happening concurrently – from grief, sadness, loss, hope, a feeling of relief and freedom, fear and possibility.

There was an underlying frustration and anger for many Yellows at the lack of acknowledgement and transparency in some of the processes, and this has led to divisions that quickly became entrenched.

Ironically, when in fact both Reds and Yellows had the same number of people appointed to the team, the impact of the handling of it all made it feel unfair, even though technically it wasn't.

The Reality post-merger was that integration was low, and there was a sense of Yellow having less status and impact than Red.

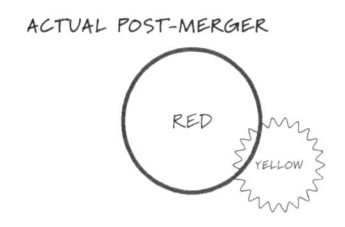

ACTUAL POST-MERGER

Failure to gel as a team led to slower delivery times and a struggle to maintain standards. Instead of becoming more efficient, the opposite seemed to be happening. No one was fully appreciating why this was. Ultimately, Red's CFO found it too much and also left.

It may seem unsalvageable but there was ultimately a Brighter Beginning. A leader came in who recognized that Red and Yellow had not fully merged, and they needed to become a new Team Orange.

With the help of external facilitators and coaches for neutrality and confidentiality, the new leader got to the heart of what had happened. Despite time having passed and people having left, they led the teams to fully acknowledge all the missed opportunities during the merger, and the impact those missed opportunities had had. They took responsibility as the new leader, despite not having been there at the time. Having done all that work and participated collectively in a Ritual as the new Team Orange, the team was energized to work together using their new ways of working. They are now thriving.

Post-intervention we can see that the impact is a significant move towards the post-merger Reality they had originally anticipated. There is now a strong foundation for achieving that ultimate goal of full integration.

GOOD BYE POST-MERGER

(ORANGE)

It's easy to see how organizations can find themselves divided in the way that Red and Yellow did. Without paying attention to the Endings that relate to their former teams or organizations, people can quickly see themselves as winners and losers. We have simplified this, because the Reality usually is that ultimately, if not immediately, both sides can feel upset. Without acknowledgement of this, it leaves its mark and people can become entrenched in their feelings and silos.

Use pain as a Stepping stone, not a campground.
Alan Cohen

We have seen real examples where this polarized experience is what has been happening, although more often there are good and bad experiences on both sides.

To illustrate this whole example of a merger further, here are some examples of the Red and Yellow experience through the lens of the Four Steps.

Reality

RED EXPERIENCE	YELLOW EXPERIENCE
Leaders communicated the projected team numbers and redundancy figures. These figures, as well as the timeline for the process of applying for roles in the newly formed team, was shared in a transparent and timely way. Red's HQ had a display in the foyer that documented the history of Red as a company, and the building, and the new layout and branding that was coming as part of the merger. Yellow was acknowledged as joining the company, but their history was not documented and celebrated in the same way. Staff surveys gave Red employees an opportunity to share thoughts about the refurbishment's designs.	Assumptions were made that Yellows had had the same information as Reds, prior to their CFO leaving. This hadn't been the case. Yellows were later to understanding the process for applying for the roles in the newly formed team and had to ask to find out the numbers of roles available. Information was shared transparently with them, but they had access to it later than Reds, and it came in fits and starts in response to questions, rather than with clarity and structure. Yellows 'knew' that they would be leaving their building. The displays had not been replicated in their foyer and when they visited Red HQ they felt like visitors, rather than part of the new organization. No senior leaders addressed the closing of the HQ directly. Their fear was that Yellow employees would be demotivated or distracted by knowing they would be moving, and they didn't want to confirm it until they were clearer on a date.

Emotions	
At Red HQ the senior leaders worked with coaches and facilitators to air their thoughts and feelings and to think through potential challenges and pitfalls of merging. Leaders replicated these conversations with their teams. Using the Emotions exercise on page 89 meant that these feelings were aired, and in doing so the intensity was dissipated and a more empathetic way of thinking emerged. This led to a conversation about a sensitivity to how incoming Yellows might feel and how they wanted them to feel, and therefore what they wanted to do to welcome them and to foster collaboration rather than silo.	The resistance that Yellows were feeling towards the Reds, and the lack of discussion or acknowledgement about how people were feeling, meant that feelings were only aired in the pub and added to feelings of 'us' and 'them'. Their leader had departed so there was no role modelling and no one to lead them through an Emotions process. The welcome that came from the Reds was met with caution and scepticism, and in turn Reds felt confused and frustrated by Yellows' apparent lack of willingness to bond as a team.
Accomplishments	
The Red team had been taken out by the CFO as she secured the new role, and she chose to thank them for their support through the merger and ask for their support whatever their position was going forward into the new organization. This was heartfelt and much appreciated.	The Yellows felt that along with the departure of their CFO, they were also losing the understanding of their strengths and contribution at line management level. There wasn't a process through which they and their leader could ensure that the incoming CFO was fully aware of their experience, achievements and strengths. As individuals, and as teams, many felt that projects and services they had been contributing to were being lost in the rush to become one team. This was exacerbating the feeling of being undervalued.

Ritual	
There was more energy in the Red team as they had a last team meeting, where they all shared stories and memories of their time together.	For the Yellow team there had been no clear date or delineation in this slow transition, and many felt the loss of the opportunity to say Good Bye to friends and colleagues, and to ways of working. In waiting for their old CFO to get in touch, they had quietly gone their separate ways. There was a lethargy and a lack of energy to organize anything.

Consider: *What opportunities were missed?*

What resonates from your own experiences?

Where and how have you observed leaders navigate these challenges of merger better?

Looking back to look forward

LOOKING BACK

In this chapter, we have covered:

- Four Steps (Reality, Emotions, Accomplishments and Ritual) brought to life with stories
- Illustrating different people Good Byes: promotion, parental leave, redundancy and retirement
- Everyday, perhaps overlooked, Endings
- Multi-faceted Endings, brought to life by the merger story of the Red and Yellow organizations as they struggled to become Orange.

TO LOOK FORWARD

In the next chapter we will cover:

- Brighter Beginnings
- A reflection on our own Ending, of completing writing 'Good Bye'
- A more detailed introduction to our Giants
- One final exercise for you.

```
┌─────────────────────────┐
│ RITUAL                  │
├───────────────────────────┐
│ ACCOMPLISHMENTS           │
├─────────────────────────────┐
│ EMOTIONS                    │
├───────────────────────────────┐
│ REALITY                       │
└───────────────────────────────┘
```

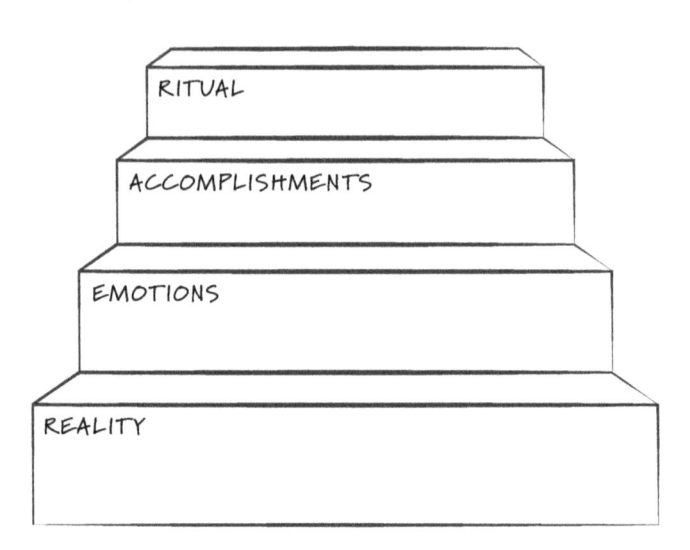

Chapter 7

Brighter Beginnings

Do the best you can until you know better. Then when you know better, do better.

Dr Maya Angelou

Remember, the whole point of Good Bye is that attending to Endings creates Brighter Beginnings. With Brighter Beginnings comes energy, confidence, deeper relationships, trust, understanding of self, better decision-making, resilience, alignment and the knowledge that the future can be navigated resourcefully.

We end this book as we began, acknowledging the myriad of Endings that carry within them an opportunity to ensure that there is an appropriate Good Bye to facilitate a healthy hello.

Our aim was to start a conversation.

And to support that conversation with some structure in the form of the REAR Four Steps. From there, our exercises were designed to give you the confidence to approach and climb those Steps for yourself and alongside those you lead.

Having acknowledged and understood more about Endings, and separated out and disentangled the elements, the leaders we have worked with have created space and gone towards the conversations that needed to happen.

We hope that however much or little you dip your toe in, this is going to start conversations for you.

In giving yourself the opportunity to process and prepare, having acknowledged and grounded your own feelings, you will be more able to be available to and open to others, and more resilient and resourced to take the Steps towards more, and Brighter, Beginnings.

Chapter 8

Good Bye, Dear Reader

Our intention was to start a conversation about Endings. We are so proud to have done so.

Thank you for coming with us. We wish you well in your Endings and Beginnings.

As we end the process of writing this book, we are doing what we have been asking you to do, and using the REAR Four Steps to say Good Bye to writing this book, and hello to putting it into the world, and all that comes with that.

Use this QR code to listen in to our Good Bye to Good Bye.

Sunsets are proof that endings can often be beautiful too.

Beau Taplin

Chapter 9

Standing on the shoulders of Giants

$$\pi$$

If I have seen further (than others) it is by standing on the shoulders of giants.

Sir Isaac Newton, 1675

We have signalled references to our Giants throughout this book with a π.

As practitioners, coaches and now authors, we are constantly learning with each other. Our work on Endings came out of one of our many energetic and energizing conversations. Alison was exploring Endings from a systemic perspective as she was also experiencing many personal Endings, and Lizzie was exploring Endings in the context of coaching and how we close coaching relationships more effectively. As we developed our ideas, we often turned to our Giants – the people whose thoughts, work and practice have most heavily influenced our own thinking and practice.

Our Giants are an important source of inspiration and along with hundreds of client conversations, and our own reflections and ideas, have formed the foundations of this work. Our Giants represent many diverse sources and disciplines, from emotional intelligence to systemic constellations, from loss and grief therapy to coaching in organizations. And particularly the seminal work of William Bridges on transitions. By standing on these shoulders, building on and synthesizing from all these great sources, we believe we have created something that is meaningful, useful and groundbreaking in its application in organizations.

Our intention for this chapter is to provide a home for all our Giants to live together, and a starting point for you to find out more about them. We'll share a short summary of their work, and how it has contributed to our work and the genesis of the concept of this book. In our conversations together we often cannot remember the origin of where an idea we are building on started. And it is part of our values to honour what has come before us, to give it full attribution, a place in history, and in our personal history. So, if we have forgotten any of our many influences, we apologize; it is not intentional.

If our work has been a starting point for you, we would be grateful if you would refer to Good Bye, and to the origins of Good Bye, as well as to us, when you share it.

William Bridges

Good Bye would not exist without William Bridges, whose book, *Managing Transitions*, addressed the human side of change, rather than looking at it from a mechanistic way. He was the first to distinguish the difference between change and transition, and name the psychological elements that were essential to understand and work with in order to take people with you on the journey of change.

In it he identifies the need to attend to Endings before entering what he calls the neutral zone before looking towards new Beginnings. He encourages us to turn back before we turn forward.

> *Beginnings depend on Endings. The problem is people don't like Endings.*
>
> William Bridges

Good Bye is the guiderail for the people who don't like Endings.

Coaching

We are coaches by profession, and incorporating both the support of our clients, and challenging them to explore what else might be possible, are hallmarks of our practice. We challenge individuals and teams to pay attention to what they might be missing, including how they could have navigated Endings better.

Coaching is forward focused. When people are caught up in an Ending, they often feel held back or they struggle to make changes they can see are necessary. Our experience is that not attending fully to what has ended is often a factor in an interruption to the forward momentum.

There are many Giants in this field, including Tim Gallwey, Laura Whitworth, Karen Kimsey-House, Henry

Kimsey-House, Phillip Sandahl, David Clutterbuck, Elaine Cox, John Blakey, Ian Day, Connie Zweig and Jonathan Passmore.

We are eternally grateful to our Giants that we have had the privilege of learning directly with: Colin Brett, Philip Brew, Roger Schwarz, Hilary Cochrane, Yvette Elcock, Karyn Prentice, Katie Friedman, Alex Campbell, Karen Dean and Tamsin Hartley.

Good Bye gives leaders and coaches a coaching-based framework for attending to past, present and future Endings.

Systemic constellations

We have spent significant time learning from systemic practitioners: Giants like John Whittington, Ty Francis, Lynn Stoney and Klaus Horn who are thought leaders and practitioners who have brought the work of Burt Hellinger into organizations and we have been privileged to learn directly from. Alongside our fellow systemic constellation students, we have never failed to be amazed by the illuminating and acknowledging power of paying attention to the system and all its parts.

We have been witness to the impact when someone leaves an organization without that being fully acknowledged. It was seeing those experiences and the shadow they cast on individuals and organizations, as well as how much better it got when we looked at and acknowledged it, that were the basis of many of the early conversations we had about this work. When somebody has left, they still have an impact. The way they leave shapes that impact.

> *Everyone who belongs to a system, must be allowed to belong – even those who have been dismissed.*
> Klaus P. Horn/Regine Brick

Good Bye seeks to offer a way of taking care of everyone in the system, past, present and future; it makes the organization, and the individuals within it, more likely to thrive.

Inclusion

Inclusion is the appreciation that all lived experiences are different and are impacted by intersectionality of our characteristics and lived-experience characteristics. Without awareness of this we can be blind to the impact decisions, culture and events are having on our teams. This also relates to the psychological safety of being able to express that impact. What means a lot to one, may not mean a lot to another. Making an Ending a Good Bye helps remind us of differences in experience and gives us a framework for exploring those differences. The way an Ending is acknowledged can be different across cultures and in missing an opportunity to meet a need, or recognize a preference in how something ends, you are missing an opportunity to make your Good Bye inclusive.

We recommend the work of Dr Dwight Turner, Shereen Daniels, Frances Frei and Anne Morris, Jenara Nerenberg, LaTonya Wilkins and Sonny Jane Wise in relation to inclusion in organizations.

Transactional Analysis

Transactional Analysis (TA) is a psychological framework that examines human interactions and communication. The Giants of the TA world we are particularly grateful to having learned directly with are Trudi Newton, Sari Van Poelje, Giles Barrow, Debbie Robinson and Karen Pratt.

As practitioners, TA is really important to our work, because it provides insights into the dynamics of personal and professional relationships. TA explores the three ego states – the Parent, Adult and Child – and how they influence our thoughts, feelings and behaviours. Understanding these states helps identify how people communicate and respond to one another. Adult to adult conversations have been a reference point for us time and again as we have thought about the best way to have the important, and sometimes difficult, conversations that are part of a Good Bye. In TA, 'strokes' are units of recognition that people give and receive to maintain social relationships, highlighting the need for acknowledgement and validation. The Drama Triangle is another key concept, illustrating the roles of Victim, Persecutor and Rescuer in conflict and everyday interactions. These roles show up time and time again in our Endings work and we often refer to them in our work with clients.

The recognition of these roles in a Good Bye helps leaders to recognize and alter unhealthy interaction patterns, promoting more constructive and fulfilling relationships, and better Good Byes.

Brené Brown

Brené Brown, a research professor at the University of Houston, introduced millions of people, including us, to the concept of vulnerability in leadership. Before her record-breaking TED talk, no leader, manager or organization was talking about this most delicate of feelings. She believes that leaders who show more vulnerability create more trusting, safe and compassionate workplaces, where all can thrive. *Daring Greatly*, Brown's second of five bestsellers, is a book that profoundly influenced our approach. Inspired by the words of Theodore Roosevelt's 'Man in the Arena' speech in 1910, Brené Brown's work encourages and equips leaders to embrace their shortcomings and acknowledge their vulnerabilities; it's better to try than to ignore. We are daring leaders to be in the arena of acknowledging Endings and being willing to be vulnerable and perhaps uncomfortable in order to lead brighter, better futures.

> *Embracing our vulnerabilities is risky but not nearly as dangerous as giving up on love and belonging and joy.*
> Brené Brown

Good Bye offers a structured way for a leader to first look at their own feelings about an Ending and then lead their team, whilst acknowledging all parties' vulnerabilities.

Grief and loss

The world of therapy, and all the world's religions and faiths, have much wisdom to offer about loss and grief. They also offer practices and Rituals that enable us to manage the inevitable loss that is part of life. Though our work is not intended to be applied to the loss of a loved one or colleague, our work has been hugely informed by our own experience of loss, and some really useful texts on this subject. From the seminal work of Elizabeth Kübler-Ross, who introduced the notion of time allowing us to move through different stages, to *The Grief Recovery Handbook* by John W. James and Russell Friedman, which offers practices to work through a loss, and your relationship to it.

> *Loss is inevitable. Sometimes loss is even predictable. In spite of these truths, we receive no formal training in how to respond to events that are guaranteed to happen and sure to cause pain and disruption.*
> John W. James and Russell Friedman

As we acknowledge on page 15, this is not a book intended for supporting colleagues who have experienced a bereavement. A starting place for support with this is your Employee Assistance Programme, if you are fortunate enough to have one. To read more about supporting colleagues through bereavement, we recommend the work of Dr Kathryn Mannix, Julia Samuel and Dr Lucy Hone. If you need help right now, organizations such as Mind, BetterHelp and The Samaritans in the UK are good places to turn.

Good Bye invites leaders to pause, take time, find the right time and acknowledge that an Ending may carry a sense of loss for themselves or a team member.

Emotional Intelligence

Emotional Intelligence refers to the ability to understand and regulate our emotional selves and build relationship and connection with others. As EQ (Emotional Quotient) became as important, if not more so, than other more traditional measures such as IQ, the understanding of leadership took a massive leap forward. We agree that EQ is key to leadership, and it is the substance of much of the work we do with our clients.

Psychologist and scientific journalist, Daniel Goleman, popularized the concept of emotional intelligence in his 1995 book *Emotional Intelligence*.

> *All learning has an emotional base.*
>
> Plato

Good Bye firstly gives a guiderail to help a leader self-regulate and understand what is going on for them, and then offers practical guides to help others to navigate their emotional responses to an Ending.

Psychological safety

You will have heard the word safety a lot in this book. And if you work with us, you will hear us say it often too. Our collective understanding of safety in the workplace as a psychological dimension (as opposed to the 'Health and Safety' physical dimension) has been led by Amy Edmonson and relates to the feeling of knowing that you will not be punished or disadvantaged by speaking up. It is a marker and measure of organizational health and high performing teams.

> *Psychological safety is not at odds with having tough conversations – it is what allows us to have tough conversations.*
>
> Amy Edmonson

Good Bye both creates and relies on safety, and we ask leaders to pay attention to all the Steps, and to go first, in order to establish and sustain that safety.

Susan Scott

Susan Scott's books *Fierce Conversations* and *Fierce Leadership* have influenced our work and thinking since we began practising as Executive Coaches. The fierceness isn't a reference to heated conversations, it's a reference to courageous ones. Her guiding principle that every conversation matters is one that is so simple, and impossible to argue with. Beneath it lies layers and layers of the depth and breadth of complexity that feature in any conversation. In her work, she offers ways to prepare for and interact during conversations. She says, 'the most valuable thing any of us can do is find a way to say the things that can't be said'. For us, conversations about Endings are the epitome of Fierce Conversations.

Nancy Kline

Nancy Kline is a pioneer of space and time. Not the outer space and astrophysics kind, but the time we allow for others to think and speak, and the space we create and hold that enables them to do that. A Good Bye requires space and time, and an understanding of the skills and practices that will support you to do that. We highly recommend her work for insights into the leadership behaviours that will support you in this work, as well as for more examples of brilliant questions you can use. We have acknowledged throughout this book that what we are suggesting requires time and space, and can perhaps feel counterintuitive amid the busyness of life at work. But as Nancy says, 'Most of the time, being, with no rush, is what produces results'.

Susan David

Susan David's work on Emotional Agility helps us not only acknowledge our Emotions, but more importantly unhook from unhelpful patterns of thoughts and behaviours. She illustrates the power of facing into our Emotions, rather than avoiding them. She also talks about Emotions as a Full Colour palette, acknowledging that we can feel many different Emotions, sometimes concurrently. David shows us that the bottling of unwanted Emotions is usually done with the best of intentions, or perhaps even out of our awareness, but 'really they have just gone underground'.

Pain and love are two sides of the same coin. In working with Emotions, we can loosen the hold an event or experience might have over us and move forward with more agility. 'This is the irony of bottling. It feels like it gives us control, but actually denies us control'.

The Emotions Step of the Good Bye process where we offer ways to work through your own feelings, and then facilitate what might be going on for others, is the heart of the work. It helps leaders to be emotionally agile, to not be afraid to acknowledge that many Emotions may be present concurrently, and to process them in order to move towards a Brighter Beginning.

David Rock

David Rock's work explores how our brains experience the workplace 'first and foremost as a social system' and how we experience and navigate threat and reward situations and responses. He is, like us, an advocate for self-awareness as the starting point for better leadership.

His SCARF model that notes the ways in which our threat and reward responses are ignited is one that we have used many times with clients as a scaffold for understanding the impact of an Ending. An Ending, particularly one that is unwelcome or painful, is bound to impact on our SCARF (Status, Certainty, Autonomy, Relatedness and Fairness).

> *Perhaps the greatest challenge facing leaders of business or government is to create the kind of atmosphere that promotes status, certainty, autonomy, relatedness and fairness.*
>
> David Rock

Good Bye shows us how we can recognize the reward of going towards what on the surface appears to be the discomfort or threat of an Ending.

Positive Psychology

In 1999, Martin Seligman first called for a broadening of the scope of psychology to place more attention in both research and practice on what is well and flourishing. Since then, the field of Positive Psychology has grown immensely in its scope and reach and has included significant breadth and depth of research and practise relating to wellbeing in the workplace, which is, after all, where many of us spend a significant portion of our lives. Scholars and practitioners including, but far from limited to, Christopher Peterson, Tim Lomas and Kate Hefferon have been instrumental in bringing Positive Psychology to the workplace. The encouragement to look at, and work at, what's well in our lives is not at the expense of acknowledging challenge, trauma or struggle. We are personally particularly grateful to Dr Lucy Ryan, Marian Rosefield and Candan Ertubey.

> *Psychology is not just a study of weakness and damage; it is also the study of strengths and virtues. Treatment is not just fixing what is broken, it is nurturing what is best within us.*
>
> Martin Seligman

Good Bye is our framework for acknowledging the full range of experience in both an Ending and a Beginning in order to facilitate better organizational and individual wellbeing.

Ending with a line of wisdom to yourself

This book is an invitation to pause, and lead Endings better.

> *Between stimulus and response there is a space. In that space is our power to choose our response. In our response lies our growth and freedom.*
> Viktor E. Frankl

A wonderful way to mark the end of the work you have done on Endings using this book is to use Exercise 15 (which we used to generate ideas for Rituals) as a Ritual in itself.

Exercise 28: A line of wisdom to yourself

For this exercise you will need a timer and some paper.

Put this question at the top:

What is important to you about a Good Bye?

Set a timer for three minutes and write or draw without stopping. This doesn't have to make sense or be well crafted. It's about getting your thoughts down on paper in a stream of consciousness.

After the three minutes is up, take a minute to look at what you have written and circle three words or short phrases that feel important to you. Don't overthink it – go with your gut.

Now set another timer and repeat the stream of consciousness, this time using your three circled words as the starting point.

After three minutes do the same as before, and circle three words, phrases or images that feel important.

Now write for a final three minutes about those words.

Finally, circle or underline three more words or phrases.

Now look back through all the words you have highlighted.

Take a final minute to write a line of wisdom or advice to yourself about what you have noticed about what is important to you about a Good Bye.

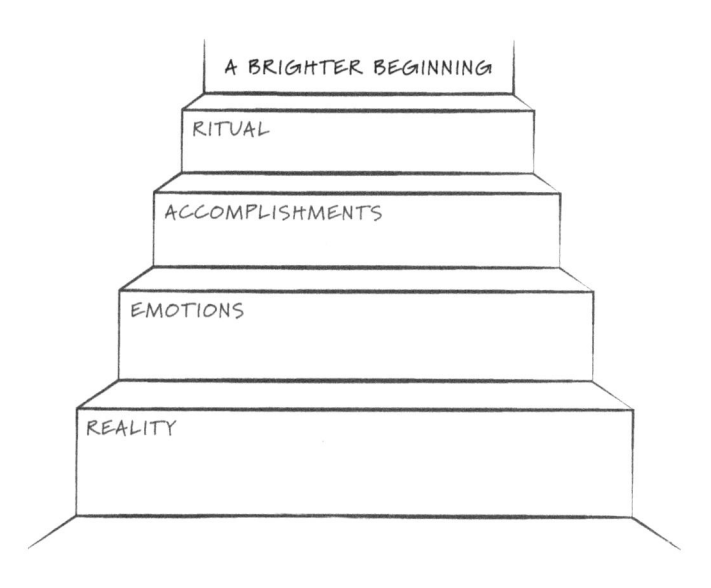

A BRIGHTER BEGINNING

RITUAL

ACCOMPLISHMENTS

EMOTIONS

REALITY

Resources

Use these QR codes to head to our website where you'll find our blog posts, podcasts, exercises and the original article that was the Beginning of Good Bye. You'll also find our Good Bye facilitation kit.

Books

Benson, Jarlath F. *Working More Creatively with Groups*. 4th Edition. Routledge, 2019.

Bridges, William, with Susan Bridges. *Managing Transitions: Making the Most of Change*. 4th Edition. John Murray Business, 2017.

Brown, Brené. *Dare to Lead: Brave Work. Tough Conversations. Whole Hearts*. 1st edition. Vermilion, 2018.

Brown, Brené. *Daring Greatly: How the Courage to be Vulnerable Transforms the Way We Live, Love, Parent and Lead*. Penguin, 2015.

Brown, Brené. *The Gifts of Imperfection: Let Go of Who You Think You're Supposed to Be and Embrace Who You Are.* Simon and Schuster, 2010.

Cameron, Julia. *The Artist's Way: Morning Pages Journal – A Companion Volume to the Artist's Way.* Hay House UK Ltd, 2017.

Cameron, Kim S. *Positively Energizing Leadership: Virtuous Actions and Relationships That Create High Performance.* Berrett-Koehler Publishers, 2021.

Charan, Ram, Stephen J. Drotter and James L. Noel. *The Leadership Pipeline: How to Build the Leadership Powered Company.* 2nd Edition. Jossey-Bass, 2011.

Cox, Elaine, Tatiana Bachkirova and David Clutterbuck, eds. *The Complete Handbook of Coaching.* 4th Edition. SAGE, 2024.

Daniels, Shereen. *The Anti-Racist Organization: Dismantling Systemic Racism In The Workplace.* Wiley, 2022.

David, Susan A. *Emotional Agility: Get Unstuck, Embrace Change, and Thrive in Work and Life.* Penguin Life, 2017.

Devine, Megan. *It's OK That You're Not OK: Meeting Grief and Loss in a Culture That Doesn't Understand.* Sounds True, 2017.

Dutton, Jane E. *Energize Your Workplace: How to Create and Sustain High-Quality Connections at Work.* 1st Edition. University of Michigan Business School Management Series. Jossey-Bass, 2003.

Dutton, Jane E., Gretchen M. Spreitzer and Shawn Achor. *How to Be a Positive Leader: Small Actions, Big Impact.* Berrett-Koehler Publishers, Incorporated, 2014.

Edmondson, Amy C. *The Fearless Organization: Creating Psychological Safety in the Workplace for Learning, Innovation, and Growth.* John Wiley & Sons, Inc, 2019.

Frei, Frances & Morriss, Anne. *Unleashed: The Unapologetic Leader's Guide to Empowering Everyone Around You.* Harvard Business Review Press, 2020.

Goleman, Daniel. *Emotional Intelligence: Why It Can Matter More Than IQ.* 25th Anniversary Edition. Bloomsbury, 2020.

Hart, Rona. *Positive Psychology: The Basics.* Taylor & Francis Group, 2020.

Hone, Lucy. *Resilient Grieving: How to Find Your Way through Devastating Loss.* Updated and Expanded 2nd Edition. The Experiment, 2024.

Ingerman, Sandra. *The Book of Ceremony: Shamanic Wisdom for Invoking the Sacred in Everyday Life.* Sounds True, 2018.

James, John W. and Russell Friedman. *The Grief Recovery Handbook: The Action Program for Moving beyond Death, Divorce, and Other Losses Including Health Career, and Faith.* 20th Anniversary Expanded Edition. Collins Living, 2009.

Kerr, James M. *Legacy: 15 Lessons in Leadership: What the All Blacks Can Teach about the Business of Life.* Constable, 2020.

Kline, Nancy. *Time to Think: Listening to Ignite the Human Mind*. Business Personal Development. Cassell Illustrated, 2014.

Kübler-Ross, Elisabeth and Kessler, David. *On Grief and Grieving: Finding the Meaning of Grief Through the Five Stages of Loss*. Simon & Schuster UK, 2014.

Mannix, Kathryn. *Listen: How to Find the Words for Tender Conversations*. William Collins, 2021.

Nerenberg, Jenara. *Divergent Mind: Thriving in a World That Wasn't Designed for You*. 1st Edition. HarperOne, 2020.

Ozenc, Kursat and Margaret Hagan. *Rituals for Work: 50 Ways to Create Engagement, Shared Purpose, and a Culture That Can Adapt to Change*. Wiley, 2019.

Parker, Priya. *The Art of Gathering: Why We Meet and Why it Matters*. Penguin Books, 2018.

Rock, David. *Quiet Leadership: Six Steps to Transforming Performance at Work; Help People Think Better – Don't Tell Them What to Do!* Paperback ed., [Nachdr.]. HarperCollins, n.d.

Rowland, Deborah. *Still Moving: How to Lead Mindful Change*. Wiley Blackwell, 2017.

Samuel, Julia. *Grief Works: Stories of Life, Death and Surviving*. Penguin Life, 2018.

Scott, Susan. *Fierce Conversations: Achieving Success at Work & in Life, One Conversation at a Time*. Revised and Updated Edition. Piatkus, 2017.

Scott, Susan. *Fierce Leadership: A Bold Alternative to the Worst "Best" Practices of Business Today.* Piatkus, 2011.

Turner, Dwight. *Intersections of Privilege and Otherness in Counselling and Psychotherapy: Mockingbird.* Routledge, 2021.

Waldo Emerson, Ralph. *Self-Reliance.* Essay, 1841.

Wilkins, LaTonya. *Leading Below The Surface: How to Build Real (and Psychologically Safe) Relationships with People Who Are Different From You.* Academy Press, 2021.

Whittington, John. *Systemic Coaching and Constellations: The Principles, Practices and Application for Individuals, Teams and Groups.* 3rd edition. Kogan Page, 2020.

Wise, Sonny Jane. *We're All Neurodiverse.* Jessica Kingsley, 2024.

Zweig, Connie. *The Inner Work of Age: Shifting from Role to Soul.* Park Street Press, 2021.

Articles

Jainish Patel and Prittesh Patel. 2019. Consequences of Repression of Emotion: Physical Health, Mental Health and General Well Being. *International Journal of Psychotherapy Practice and Research*, 1(3):16–21.

Guy-Evans and Olivia Fight. 2023. Flight, Freeze or Fawn: How We Respond to Threats. *Simply Psychology, Simply Scholar Ltd.*

Lawler III, Edward. 2002. The Folly of Forced Ranking. *Strategy & Business, Third Quarter 2002 – Issue 28.*

Rock, David. 2009. Managing With the Brain in Mind. *Strategy & Business, Autumn 2009 – Issue 56.*

Other

James Cascio, BANI:A Framework for Understanding A Turbulent World: https://ageofbani.com/

Jurgen Klopp Interview: www.youtube.com/watch?v=-dcbhxJ2lzw

www.mind.org.uk

www.betterhelp.com

www.samaritans.org or call (free in UK) 116 123

REAR

RITUAL

ACCOMPLISHMENTS

EMOTIONS

REALITY

Exercises

1. Bring current Endings into focus
2. What is resonating for you?
3. Beginnings get a lot of attention
4. What Endings are occurring?
5. The value of attending to Endings
6. Charting your relationship with Endings at work
7. Tune into your nervous system
8. A deeper dive into the Endings happening now
9. Using a metaphor to bring Reality to life
10. Get in contact with all that you are feeling
11. Acknowledge the losses you are experiencing
12. Own what you have Accomplished
13. Channel your cheerleaders
14. Exploring Ritual possibilities that resonate for you
15. Creative ways to generate ideas for your Ritual
16. Listen better!
17. Preparing yourself to listen
18. Being present – getting back in the room
19. Listening as a team

20. Think through the relationship between you, others and the Ending
21. Agree ground rules before you embark
22. Two sticky-note ways to use SCARF
23. Exploring Emotions together
24. It only takes a minute
25. Opening the door to the new beginning
26. Create the heartfelt leaving speech you would like to receive
27. The standing Ending
28. A line of wisdom to yourself

Endings stories

An all too common tale – William's story

I loved you. You loved me. We'll all be ok. – Jürgen Klopp's story

Too easily discarded – Kim's story

Building belonging – Itsuki's story

Taking the later train – Isobel's story

Who am I now? – Björn's story

How dare you – Maddy's story

Still haunted – Anisa's story

Sweat the small stuff – Elif's story

Making thank you meaningful – a team story

Mugs and moustaches

Timely tidying

The final curtain

Rushed re-structuring – Priya and Rohan's story

What do you do?

Defeat from the jaws of victory – Jacqueline's story

I don't drink coffee! – Paul's story

Hadrian's Wall

Moving out

Using where it happened to honour what happened

The wedding speech

A class act – Lucy's story

Retirement done well – Rahat's story

No time to pause – Anna's story

Red and yellow don't always make orange

Good Bye, Dear Reader – Lizzie and Alison's story

Acknowledgements

Alison

To my husband Phil, for quietly looking after me always and encouraging me to pursue whatever I wanted, as long as it made me happy. To my mum Judith, for teaching me to be an independent, curious thinker. To my children Ellen, Matthew and Ruth, who are already Giants and are my constant source of inspiration and hope. To my siblings John, Sue and Helen, and siblings-in-law Alyson and Gill. Everyday our glorious extended family brings me joy.

To my loved ones who are no longer with me, who taught me about the pain of loss and unconditional love. Jack and Nellie, Aunty Caroline, my wonderful parents-in-law Ann and Eric and my lovely dad Peter, my Giant.

To Ladies What Lunch, who have travelled with me professionally and personally forever: Sue, Mary and Sue.

To all my clients who I've had the privilege to work alongside in their leadership journey. I learn from you every day.

To Kelly, Jess, Caroline, Wendy and Sara; all my friends who have become colleagues, and colleagues who have become friends who have encouraged and supported us in publishing *Good Bye*.

To Lizzie – it's been the best of adventures. Thank you, dear friend.

Lizzie

To Craig, for love, music, travel, food, tea, support and making all this, and so much more, possible. AYW

To Jack and Dylan, for inspiring everything I do.

I am blessed with family that are friends and friends that are family. I am so grateful to have you all in my life, enriching it every day.

To my Mum, and to my treasured siblings and your wonderful spouses and beautiful families. I am incredibly grateful both to you and for you.

To Zoë and your gorgeous ones, for absolutely bloody everything frankly.

To Claire and Jon, Jo and Bill, Mel and Piers, Sally and Mike and all your lovelies, for all the love and laughs.

To the lifelong and treasured fun and friendship of the Durham Dolls, the 'avin a laughs and the TWAS team, especially our Lucy by the sea.

To my many musical families over the years, especially Gemma for bringing the music back.

To the fabulous friends who happen to also be colleagues that I have learned from and laughed with every time I see them, especially Caroline, Yvette, Sarah, Rakhee, Sara, Afsar, Sam, Wendy, Debra, Katie and Alex.

To Ian Collins and Mary Marsh for your lessons in life and leadership and the generosity that has stayed with me.

To Victoria, Valerie, Lisa, Russell, Caroline, Lizzie, Jasmine, Elizabeth, all the amazing Cornwallis folk and the teams

I've yet to meet as I write this, for your care, skill, kindness and for the priceless gift of the future. My gratitude is beyond measure.

To the wonderful clients I learn from every day – how fortunate I am to do a job I love this much.

And to the class of 2004 and my fellow teacher travellers, I was so lucky to do that job too. You continue to inspire me.

To Ali, this has been the most extraordinary journey and you are the very best companion for it, my dear friend. Cheers to us and what we have accomplished and here's to what's next.

Together

For getting this book out of our heads and into your hands, together we want to share our deep appreciation of:

Clients and friends who have generously shared their stories and whose work with us has inspired this book.

Kate Sims for illustrations, making sense of our ideas and scribblings and making our book and website beautiful.

Jess Meyer Rassow, we have found it hard to summarize what you have brought to this whole process. It's a lot! The answer we have given each other to many of our questions has been 'Let's ask Jess!'. Thank you for always finding the answers.

Shoshana Boyd-Gelfand, Amy Braier, Wendy Bedborough and Ellen Lucas for being the best of Beta readers and adding such valuable insights as well as a keen eye for detail.

Kelly Holland, Sam Filsell and Sam Smith for keeping the Randolph Partnership and Causeway Coaching running smoothly when we've hidden away to write, and for all your years of support of our businesses.

John Cushing and Michael Weadock from Anything But Footy podcasts for your brilliant production and endless patience.

Iona Lawrence for your companionship and enthusiasm for our work as a fellow Endings traveller.

Alison Jones for turning a 'maybe we could write a book' into a belief that we could, followed by the guidance – and deadlines! – we needed to finish our book.

The Practical Inspiration Publishing Team: Michelle Charman, Shell Cooper, Nim Moorthy, Susannah Fountain, Emily Boyd and Kelly Winter for support, for the cover that we love so much, for the brilliant editing and copy editing and for helping us tell the world we wrote a book!

Index

A

Accomplishments (REAR Steps) 57–58
  leading others 121–123
  multi-faceted Endings 152
  naming 92–94
  promotion 133–134
  redundancy 137
  retirement 139, 142
  your first steps 92–94
ADHD 31
agency 83
Ali, Muhammad 93
All Blacks 62
Angelou, Maya 155
anger 37, 89, 120
Aristotle 56
Autonomy (SCARF model) 27
avoiding Endings 33–34, 44–50, 135–136

B

behaviour, impact of Endings on 22–24
Benson, Jarlath 95
betrayed, feeling 40–42
blow your own trumpet 93, 93 n6
Brick, Regine 163
Bridges, William 34, 160–161
Brighter Beginnings 20. 63–64, 155–156, 169
Brown, Brené 4, 56, 89, 165

C

Cameron, Kim 89
Cascio, Jamais 1
certainty 20–21
  SCARF model 27
challenge, work as 74–79
change, leading 69
Charan, Ram 133
coaching, Giants in 161–162
Cohen, Alan 150
compromise agreement 45, 45 n5, 84
connection, Endings an opportunity for 32–33
conversations 168
COVID-19 pandemic 46–47

D

David, Susan 56, 72, 81, 82, 169
death 15, 60
Decelerator Helpline 20, 43, 43 n4
delegating, reluctance to 132–133
denial 15–16
Devine, Megan 37, 38
Dickens, Charles 70
Dutton, Jane 92, 121
Dweck, Joseph 48

E

Edmonson, Amy 167
Eliot, T.S. v
Emerson, Ralph Waldo 48

emotional agility 69, 72, 169
emotional awareness and literacy 71–72
emotional intelligence 72, 166–167
Emotional Quotient (EQ) 167
emotional response 36–37
emotions 56, 120–121
Emotions cards 90, *119*
Emotions (REAR Steps) 55–56
  leading others 117–121
  multi-faceted Endings 152
  promotion 135
  retirement 139, 141–142
  your first steps 82, 87, 88–92
Endings
  avoiding 33–34. 44–50, 135–136
  book metaphor 84–88
  can leave scars 21–22
  different starting points 73–74, 83
  discomfort of 33
  draining and distracting 30–31
  everyday 144–145
  framework 6–7
  impact relationships and behaviour 22–24
  increase opportunity for equity 20
  less investment in 18
  lessons are learned 19
  more, not fewer 33
  not attended to 43–44, 65–66, 70
  an opportunity for connection 32–33
  perspective 19–20
  previous 98
  reduced people cost 19
  staged 73–74, 83
  standing 145
  and threat responses 26, 28–30
  and trust 24–25
  use of term 1
  why they matter 18–21
equity 20
everyday Endings 144–145
examples 8, 9
  Accomplishments (REAR Steps) 58
  connection 33
  feeling betrayed 41–42
  ghosts and entanglements 43–44
  leaving gift 125–126
  leaving places and spaces 126, 127–129
  look around for 9
  loss 38–39
  Endings done well 10, 140–141
  organizational pace 47
  poorly managed Ending 5–6
  Reality (REAR Steps) 54
  retirement well done 140–141
  red and yellow don't always make orange 147–150
  Reality book exercise 85
  restructuring 64–66
  retirement 72–73
  Ritual (REAR Steps) 61–62
  scars left by Endings 22
  silos 23–24
exercises
  1: Bring current Endings into focus 3
  2: What is resonating for you? 6

Index

3: Beginnings get a lot of attention 17
4: What Endings are occurring? 31–32
5: The value of attending to Endings 64
6: Charting your relationship with Endings at work 75–76
7: Tune into your nervous system 76–77
8: A deeper dive into Endings happening now 77–79
9: Using a metaphor to bring Reality to life 84–85
10: Get in contact with all that you are feeling 89–90
11: Acknowledging the losses you are experiencing 91–92
12: Own what you have Accomplished 94
13: Channel your cheerleaders 94
14: Exploring Ritual possibilities that resonate for you 96
15: Creative ways to generate ideas for your Ritual 96–97
16: Listening better! 103
17: Preparing yourself to listen 103–104
18: Being present – getting back in the room 104–105
19: Listening as a team 106–108
20: Think through the relationship between you, others and the Ending 112–114
21: Agree ground rules before you embark 114
22: Two sticky-note ways to use SCARF 115–116
23: Exploring Emotions together 118–120
24: It only takes a minute 122
25: Opening door to the new Beginning 124
26: Create the heartfelt leaving speech you would like to receive
27: The standing Ending 145
28: A line of wisdom to yourself

F

Facilitator's Guide 106–108
Fairness (SCARF model) 28
Fierce Conversations 168
'Fight/Flight/Freeze' 28, *29*, 76–77
fix and rescue 39–40
Forced Ranking 25
Four Fs 29–30, 76–77, 117
Four Steps of Ending *see* REAR Four Steps
Friedman, Russell 123, 166

G

General Electric 25
ghosts and entanglements 43–44
Goleman, Daniel 72, 88, 167
Good Bye, use of term 1
GoodByeCoach.co.uk 7, 106
grief *see* loss and grief
GSK 25

H
Hone, Lucy 15
Horne, Klaus B. 163

I
inclusion, Giants in 163
identity 72–73
improvise 8–9
influential works 9
Inside Out 71
International Journal of Psychotherapy and Research 35

J
James, John W 123, 166
job security 84

K
Kerr, James 62
Kline, Nancy 57, 103, 105, 109, 117, 168–169
Korzybski, Alfred 146
Kübler-Ross, Elizabeth 166

L
Lawler, Edward E. 25
leading change 69
leading others
  Accomplishments 121–122
  Emotions 117–121
  architect, messenger or victim? 112–114
  Reality 115–117
  Ritual 123–129
leaders, capacity to hold Emotion and vulnerability 36–37
leadership, crucial areas of 69–70
leaving speeches 125, 128–129
lessons learned 19
listening 101–102
loss and grief
  facing in to 37–39
  Giants in 165–166
  naming 91–92
  navigating 69

M
Mannix, Kathryn 15, 101, 103
merger and/or acquisition (M&A) 146–153
Microsoft 25
multi-faceted Good Byes 146–153

N
negativity 89
Newton, Isaac 159

O
organization
  systemic health of 22–24
  and avoiding Endings 44–50

P
pace 37
  as barrier to Endings 45–48
parental leave 138
perspective 19–20, 23
people cost, reduced 19
People Good Byes 132–144
  parental leave 138
  promotion 132–135
  redundancy 135–137
  retirement 138–144
pitching, as Ending 144–145

places and spaces, leaving 126, 127–129
Plato 55, 167
Positive Psychology 122, 170–171
positives, focusing on 35
process, as barrier to Endings 44–45
projects, as Endings 73–74
promotion 132–135
protected characteristics 28, 28 n3
psychological safety 70, 167

R

Reality (REAR Steps) 52–54
  everyday Endings 144–145
  'future Reality' 134–135
  leading others 115–117
  multi-faceted Endings 151
  promotion 133–135
  retirement 139, 140–141
REAR Four Steps (Reality, Emotions, Accomplishments and Ritual) 8–9, *12*, 16, 34, 44, 73, 109
  importance of order 64–66
  introduction to 51–52
  multi-faceted Endings 146, 151–153
  promotion 133–135
  retirement 138–143
  Step 1: Reality 52–54, 81–88, 115–117, 134–135, 139, 144–145
  Step 2: Emotions 55–56, 82, 87, 88–92, 117–121, 135, 139, 141–142, 152
  Step 3: Accomplishments 57–58, 121–123
  Step 4: Ritual 60–63, 66, 95–98, 123–129, 139–140, 143, 144–145, 153
redundancy 72, 135–137
Relatedness (SCARF model) 27–28
relationships, impact of Endings on 22–24
rescue 39–40
resilience, lack of 48
retirement 138–144
Ritual (REAR Steps) 60–63
  everyday Endings 144–145
  insincere/inappropriate 66
  leading others 123–129
  multi-faceted Endings 153
  retirement 139–140, 143
  standing Ending 145
  your first steps 95–98
retirement 2, 72
Rock, David 26, 169–170
  see also SCARF model
roles, conflicting 83–84
Roosevelt, Theodore 165
Rosenberg, Marshall B. 52

S

safety, psychological 70, 167
Samuel, Julia 15
SCARF model 26–28, 115–116, 170
scars left by Endings 21–22
Scott, Susan 103, 117, 168
self-awareness 70
Seligman, Martin 170–171
silos 23–24

space and time 8, 168–169
start with yourself *see* you go first
starting points, different from Ending points 73–74
Status (SCARF model) 26–27
strategic thinking 70
stress 28–30
systemic, use of term 22 n2
systemic constellations, Giants in 162–163
systemic thinking 70

T
Taplin, Beau 157
theatre, Rituals in 62
thinking
  strategic 70
  systemic 70
threat responses 26, 28–30
  reactions *29–30*
time and space 8, 168–169
timing 15–16
timing dissonance 83
Transactional Analysis (TA) 164
trauma 16
trauma responses 28
trust 24–25
truth, facing 35

V
vulnerability 74–79, 165

W
Welsh, Jack 25
Whittington, John 18
Windsor Leadership Trust 48
wisdom to yourself 172–173
work safely 8

Y
'yank and rank' 25
you go first 7–8
  crucial areas of leadership 69–70
  different starting and Ending points 73–74
  identity 72–73
  work my challenge you 74–79
your first steps
  Step 1: Reality: Naming it 81–88
  Step 2: Emotions 88–92
  Step 3: Accomplishments 92–94
  Step 4: Ritual 95–98

Z
Zweig, Connie 38

About the authors

Leading Executive Coaches Alison Lucas, of Randolph Partnership Ltd, and Lizzie Bentley Bowers, of The Causeway Coaching Ltd, are professionally accredited coaches and facilitators, working at board to top talent level across all sectors. Balancing clients' individual and commercial needs and outcomes, they equip leaders to thrive and to navigate change in their complex and uncertain world. Their combined decades of learning and thousands of conversations with leaders led them to Endings, an overlooked aspect of change that they have since been determined to bring into the leadership conversation. Collaboration, shared experience and shared learning is a hallmark of their practice and they enjoy and benefit from the support and challenge they offer each other. Holding the pursuit of the best outcomes for their clients lies at the heart of their collaborations. You can find out more about them at GoodByeCoach.co.uk.

A quick word from Practical Inspiration Publishing...

We hope you found this book both practical and inspiring – that's what we aim for with every book we publish.

We publish titles on topics ranging from leadership, entrepreneurship, HR and marketing to self-development and wellbeing.

Find details of all our books at: www.practicalinspiration.com

Did you know...

We can offer discounts on bulk sales of all our titles – ideal if you want to use them for training purposes, corporate giveaways or simply because you feel these ideas deserve to be shared with your network.

We can even produce bespoke versions of our books, for example with your organization's logo and/or a tailored foreword.

To discuss further, contact us on info@practicalinspiration.com.

Got an idea for a business book?

We may be able to help. Find out more about publishing in partnership with us at: bit.ly/PIpublishing.

Follow us on social media...

- @PIPTalking
- @pip_talking
- @practicalinspiration
- @piptalking
- Practical Inspiration Publishing